Do-It-Yourself
EAR TRAINING

BY CHRIS KRINGEL

2742-0237-9562-4528

ISBN 978-1-70512-653-0

Copyright © 2024 by HAL LEONARD LLC
International Copyright Secured All Rights Reserved

No part of this publication may be reproduced in any form or by
any means without the prior written permission of the Publisher.

Visit Hal Leonard Online at **www.halleonard.com**

Explore the entire family of Hal Leonard products and resources

World headquarters, contact:
Hal Leonard
7777 West Bluemound Road
Milwaukee, WI 53213
Email: info@halleonard.com

In Europe, contact:
Hal Leonard Europe Limited
Dettingen Way
Bury St Edmunds, Suffolk, IP33 3YB
Email: info@halleonardeurope.com

In Australia, contact:
Hal Leonard Australia Pty. Ltd.
4 Lentara Court
Cheltenham, Victoria, 3192 Australia
Email: info@halleonard.com.au

CONTENTS

- 4 **INTRODUCTION**
- 8 **CHAPTER 1:** Maps
- 12 **CHAPTER 2:** Listening
- 15 **CHAPTER 3:** Practice and Motivation
- 24 **CHAPTER 4:** Understanding Intervals
- 30 **CHAPTER 5:** Ear Training Template
- 36 **CHAPTER 6:** Interval Practice
- 44 **CHAPTER 7:** Scale Practice
- 49 **CHAPTER 8:** Descending Interval Practice
- 52 **CHAPTER 9:** Triad Theory and Practice
- 59 **CHAPTER 10:** Seventh Chords
- 66 **CHAPTER 11:** Rhythm
- 75 **CHAPTER 12:** Time Elements
- 84 **CHAPTER 13:** Rhythm Dictation
- 91 **CHAPTER 14:** Do-It-Yourself!
- 94 **FINAL THOUGHTS**

INTRODUCTION

Welcome to *Do-It-Yourself Ear Training*. This book is for musicians who can already read music (although some basics are included as a review) and are ready to dive deeper into the relationships among sounds that make music what it is. When you embark on a new journey, a map can be a useful tool. If you know where you want to go, a good map can help make the journey easier. If you don't know exactly where you want to go, a map is great for showing the territory. Because this is a "do-it-yourself" book, I wanted to give you the tools to create your own map for ear training. This book starts with music as the territory and offers insights and information about areas you may encounter. It explores you (the driver), the vehicle, and your relationships with the world around you. We'll look at strategies to help you with optimal performance. Then, we'll zoom in on the map and look at the locations you'll visit. We'll drive around and learn about the locations and have experiences. Finally, you will be able to review your experiences and create your own for the next visit or expedition. This book is about music, listening, motivation, practice, and ear training. I hope you enjoy the journey.

> *"If you know the way broadly you will see it in everything."*—Miyamoto Musashi

The quote above points to the art of learning; once you know what it takes to become skillful, you can become skillful at anything because it's not about the thing, it's about knowing the process. A major hurdle in any practice is the journey itself. In the do-it-yourself spirit, this book will focus on practice as the foundation of listening and ear training development.

> *"What you put into life is what you get out of it."*—Clint Eastwood

A do-it-yourself project requires some note-taking. Get a notebook, because questions will be asked, and you will want to fully participate. In the beginning, I'll take you step-by-step through each process. As the book proceeds, the exercises will evolve into a do-it-yourself motif with explanations and ideas for you to develop on your own. Chapters 1–4 are necessary to build your foundation. The earlier chapters are a setup for the do-it-yourself method, which includes listening, practice optimization, and motivation. At Chapter 4, you may jump forward to Chapter 11 and work with rhythm if you are so inclined.

ONLINE RESOURCES

On page 1, you will find a unique code. Go to **www.halleonard.com/mylibrary** and enter that code to gain access to the full audiobook, individual audio tracks, and PDF handouts, for download or streaming. Audio tracks and PDF handouts are indicated throughout the book by these symbols:

USING THE AUDIO

Several exercises in this program focus on internalizing pitch through singing. It's important to adjust the octave as needed to accommodate your vocal range. If an exercise feels too high, it's best not to strain your voice. Feel free to lower the octave and continue with the exercise.

Several of the examples will require detailed listening. I strongly recommend using headphones when listening to the audio examples to improve your focus and minimize distractions. Using headphones can enhance your detailed listening experience by allowing you to fully immerse yourself in the audio and catch subtle details that might otherwise go unnoticed.

LEARNING STEPS

Learning is the gradual development of something from simple to complex. It can be defined as a process that leads to change, as the acquisition and retention of knowledge, and as a change in performance or behavior.

How do we learn? What is the process? You can start with these three steps:

1. Receive/Take In—observe, listen, read
2. Process—analyze, memorize, experience
3. Express/Let Out—apply, perform, record, teach, compose

The steps are easy to remember; liken it to breathing: inhale (take in), hold (process), and exhale (let out). Do you use all three steps? Think about it. A lot of ideas start and end in the mind. Musical learning requires us to engage with our ears. We can read about a scale in a book and memorize a pattern on how to play it, but if we don't perform that scale or play it in a musical context, we miss out on how it sounds—we miss the "making music" part. Gaps in knowledge become very apparent after performing or trying to teach. Go through the learning steps, identify gaps, and revise.

The learning process: Watch, Think, Feel, and Do.

MINDSET

> *"Fall in love with some activity, and do it! Nobody ever figures out what life is about, and it doesn't matter. Explore the world. Nearly everything is really interesting if you go into it deeply enough. Work as hard and as much as you want on the things you like to do the best. Don't think about what you want to be, but what you want to do."*
> —Richard Feynman (Nobel Prize winner)

Make the time to get the most out of learning. Surrender yourself to the process. I think practicing isn't enjoyable for some because they are focused on the destination and make the present moment an obstacle or a hurdle they must overcome to get to the destination. Don't think that far in advance—focus on the small parts of practice and you'll eventually find yourself at the destination.

Like the seasons, learning is full of contrast. Spring brings new ideas and the promise of discovery; things feel fresh and exciting. At times, though, it can rain and be unpredictable. Along with the newness that is springing up, we still have to "rake the leaves," so to speak, so flowers can bloom. Summer is a time when life is flowing, bright, energetic, and generally consistent; though, at times, it can be too hot, uncomfortable, and unpredictable. Fall brings rapid change in either direction, and one never knows what the day will bring—leaves are falling, and you have to clean up in preparation for winter. Things are slowing down or coming to an end, and you can feel it. Winter is a time of hibernation; it's cold and nothing is changing. You might feel unmotivated, dormant, or at a plateau. Cold might be a welcome shock to the system, but the weather might keep you from exploring new things. We are part of the natural world, and we ebb and flow in much the same way. Learning and practice are full of changes; one can flow, accept, and surrender—or struggle and resist the changes in seasons.

EAR TRAINING

Ear training is a practice in which you learn to identify all aspects of music by listening. It is like dictation in language—the ability to recognize and transcribe what's being heard. Ear training and music theory work together; by knowing the theory behind what you hear, you are able to recognize, name, and understand music in a way that can open many doors for you as a musician.

Ear training is a topic that has been taught in a very logical way, one that requires a dedicated effort of listening and discerning the relationships among notes. I wanted to create a method that included:

- The Art of Listening—how we listen to the world around us
- The Mental Game of Learning—why and how we learn
- Creativity—how to use music to create and how it makes us feel
- Logic—understanding, execution, and definition

Learning how to become a better listener and having a basic understanding of how the mind works are essential to building a good foundation for any skill. Creativity reinforced with practical concepts helps cement learning in an effective, musical way. You'll find many different listening exercises in this book because my goal is to cultivate the art of listening, much like sommeliers fine-tune their taste buds for the complexities of wine.

RELATIVE PITCH AND PERFECT PITCH

Relative pitch is the ability to identify or recreate a pitch when compared to another pitch. With great relative pitch, a musician can:

- Identify *intervals* (the distance between two notes)
- Identify *chord qualities* (major, minor, etc.)
- Identify pitches between two different notes
- Recreate melodies built from a reference tone

Perfect pitch, or *absolute pitch*, is a rare ability to identify a pitch without the aid of a reference pitch. People who have perfect pitch often describe seeing a color associated with the sound or having a "knowing" sense about what they hear. It is said that learning perfect pitch later in life is not possible, but some disagree. This book focuses on relative pitch; if you are interested in perfect pitch, you can easily find information elsewhere. Though this book will still be useful to someone with perfect pitch.

MUSIC

Music is an art form that is expressed through sound and is perceived audibly (by the ears). Like most art forms, music is a way to express the intangible world of thoughts, concepts, and emotions, and bring them into the physical world by using the voice or an instrument. Music can also mimic the world around us. Instruments and voices paint pictures of the natural world. For example, a flute in a piece of music might mimic a bird's song. As life has become more urban and technology has advanced, one can see how music continues to evolve as well—the industrial age brought with it electric instruments and distortion that sounded machine-like, while the computer age brought about electronic music. As we evolve, so does our music. Music is the expression of our hearts and minds.

SPIE

Learning can be a holistic experience, a SPIE experience: **S**piritual, **P**hysical, **I**ntellectual, and **E**motional. If you think about it, these four dimensions cover our experience of life; they are the ways in which we interface with the world. The phrase "Mind, body, and spirit," is another common way in which we characterize these dimensions. Learning can fall flat when all four aspects are not present or in our consciousness. Spirituality can be considered "life purpose," "life meaning," or a connection to life itself. Physicality is how we interface with the world around us. Intellectual is how we think, understand, and solve problems. Emotion is how we feel about an experience. When we are aware of each of these aspects, we can connect to learning in a more meaningful way. It becomes less about the content and more about how we see it. Let's look at how these dimensions work in our life and musical landscape.

Spiritual

Spiritual is a broad term, and it can have many interpretations. In this book, the use of the word spiritual refers to a deeper meaning and purpose. Spiritual can be defined as a sense of purpose, direction, passion, aspiration, and impulse to action. In life and with music, one must zoom way out to look through the spiritual lens. Musicians with a strong spiritual lens are fueled by a deeper meaning; it is their connection to something bigger than self, and music is the vehicle to share this passion and purpose.

Physical

Physical is our body and the physical world around us. Physical can be defined as a physical sensation, movement, groove, sensitivity to vibration, our ears, our eyes, and all things related to matter. In life and in music, one must connect to the five senses to meet the physical dimension. How we move our body, our dexterity in playing our instrument, listening with our ears, using our voice to speak, and seeing the world around us. Some musicians have a deep connection to the body and channel their physical energy in pursuit of technical excellence or by creating and making music.

Intellectual

Intellect is our ability to reason and understand objectively. Intellect can be defined as comprehension, judgment, problem-solving, use of language, self-expression, communication, and seeing the bigger picture. In life and in music, one must have a wide range of vision to see the vast complexity that is life. Through the intellectual lens, we seek to understand, observe, solve problems, and challenge the known to expand knowledge, teach, and refine. Musicians with a strong intellectual lens are constantly expanding on the craft—the love of learning almost exceeds music itself.

Emotional

Emotional is the instinctive state of being that arises based on our interpretation of circumstances. Emotion can be defined as love, passion, sadness, anger, fear, excitement, and joy. Emotion is power, healing, expression, empathy, and relationship-based. In life and in music, emotion can be the fuel to get you where you want to go or drive you off a cliff. Through the emotional lens, we create states of being, express pain, evoke joy, and share in the rich and emotional human experience. Music is used in movies, television, commercials, videos, grocery stores, and even elevators to elicit emotion.

CHAPTER 1:
Maps

MUSIC THEORY

Music theory is the descriptive part of the language of music. It is the way music has been systematized for understanding and communication purposes. Music theory is how we describe the relationships of the tones and rhythms in music. It gives musicians the ability to convey complex ideas in a simple and universal way. Thanks to theory, a musician can see a piece of music, understand its structure, and perform it without ever having heard it before. Music theory can be likened to a map. A map describes relationships of specific features in the terrain and outlines what you'll find when exploring a specific location. There are many different types of maps that attempt to represent specific things. With a map, several musicians can meet at the same place and time and create music. Without a map, those same musicians might have to spend time discussing how to get to the location before they can create. If someone knows an area well, they can create shortcuts and show others how to navigate using a map they have created. A map is not the territory—it is a representation of the territory.

HARMONIC SERIES

The *harmonic series* originates directly from the laws of vibration; it occurs naturally and can be explained mathematically. It's the base for resonance and harmony in the natural world and is the foundation of all musical scales and tuning systems. The *harmonic series* (or *overtone series*) is a sequence of frequencies that resonate simultaneously when the *fundamental*, or lowest tone in the series, is played. These frequencies—called overtones or harmonics—sound at lower levels, some almost inaudible. Nevertheless, all are present within the fundamental tone. In the following example, a string vibrates at a frequency of 110Hz, and overtones are resonating outward.

Function	String Vibrating	Pitch	Frequency
Fundamental		A	110hz
1st overtone		A	220hz
2nd overtone		E	329.63hz
3rd overtone		A	440hz
4th overtone		C#	554.37hz
5th overtone		E	660hz
6th overtone		G	783.99hz

It is important to note the presence of these overtones in each fundamental. If you are interested in the fundamentals of pitch and the mathematical relationship between frequencies, study the harmonic series; it is a deep dive into understanding the natural world of sound.

PITCH—HIGH AND LOW (VERTICAL)

Music is made from vibrations called *sound waves*. The speed at which a sound wave vibrates is called *frequency*. Frequency is measured in hertz (Hz). The faster the vibration, the higher the frequency; the slower the vibration, the lower the frequency. In music, we use letter names to identify pitches instead of using the measured frequencies. So, letters in the *music alphabet* (A–B–C–D–E–F–G) are assigned to each pitch that vibrates at a specific frequency. Any sound that is perceived as a pitch will recur at intervals called *octaves*, where half the frequency value is lower, and double the frequency value is higher, but the pitch has a recognizable pattern. Pitch is divided into 12 notes in different octaves. It helps to visualize notes or pitches as having an up and down; they live in the vertical world, and we notate pitch on a musical staff as such. In Western music, we use a tuning standard based on the note A above middle C—which vibrates at 440 Hz. See the following chart as a reference. This is a map of pitches on a piano and the different octaves of the C note in musical notation with the corresponding frequency for each note in hertz. It also shows the frequency range of common musical instruments.

Let's look at *A440* (as the note is called). The A one octave lower is measured at 220 Hz, and the A above 440 Hz is 880 Hz.

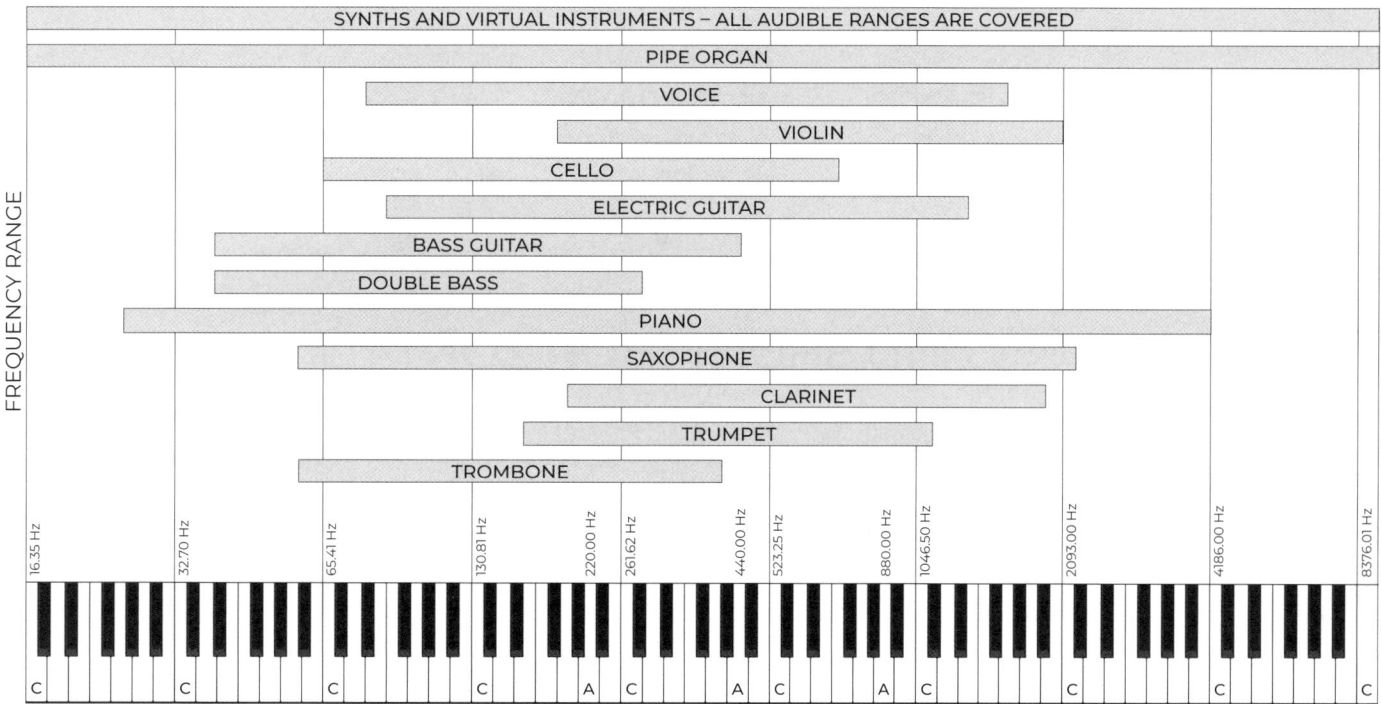

High-Low Exercise

This is an exercise for hearing pitches and identifying whether they are higher or lower by comparison. I'll play a note followed by another note. See if you can tell whether the second note is higher or lower than the first. I will use a piano sound for the first four examples and switch instruments after that for variation.

Let's begin. Is the second note higher or lower in relation to the first note?

 **TRACK 1** High-Low Quiz

INTERVALS

As mentioned in the introduction, an interval is the distance between two notes or pitches. Hearing the distance between notes, chords, and keys is a major element of ear training. Hearing intervals involves recognizing the vertical distance between two pitches. We will zoom in and out on pitch intervals in Chapter 4 and measure the distance or interval of notes as they happen in musical time in Chapter 11.

MUSICAL TIME

Musical time is the flow of time-specific, musical events. Like real-world or clock time, musical time moves forward from the past, through to the present, and into the future. When we focus our attention on the pulse or beat intervals of a musical idea, we enter into musical time—the flow, the feel, the beat, the rhythm—we synchronize with the groove. "Keeping time" is a phrase that is used often when referring to musical time. We measure musical time in relation to clock time by measuring the beats or pulses present in a musical idea. This measurement is called *tempo*.

TEMPO

Tempo (Italian for "time"), or the speed at which a piece of music is played is measured in *bpm* (beats per minute). Another way we indicate the tempo of a piece of music is by using *tempo markings* at the start of a piece. Tempo markings give an approximate tempo range for a piece of music by using adjectives—slowly, moderately, moderately fast, fast, and very fast—to describe the tempo. Most composers still use the Italian terms for tempo: largo, moderato, allegro, presto, and so on. Tempo is crucial to how a piece of music feels. Musical time is fluid and tempo can fluctuate or change based on circumstances. With the advent of modern computer technology, tempo can also be very specific and exact.

ADAGIO	ANDANTE	MODERATO	ALLEGRO	PRESTO
slowly	*walking*	*moderate*	*lively*	*quickly*
(60-80 bpm)	(80-100 bpm)	(100-120 bpm)	(120-160 bpm)	(160-200 bpm)

RHYTHM—LONG AND SHORT (HORIZONTAL)

Rhythm in music is the measurement of a grouping or series of beat intervals according to duration and accent. In musical notation, rhythm is placed on the horizontal plane of time, moving left to right. Rhythm is organized into *measures* that divide time into groups of beats. We measure time in a piece of music by using notes and rests, each having specific lengths. Reading rhythm gives us a road map to follow when creating and performing music. Rhythm is at the root of all music, its most primal and foundational aspect. Understanding rhythm is necessary for reading music, and feeling rhythm is as important as hearing pitch. Hearing and interpreting rhythm is another part of ear training. We will go down that road in Chapter 11.

VOLUME

Volume is best described as the intensity of a sound. It is a combination of the amplitude and frequency of a sound wave. *Amplitude* is a measurement of the amount of change in air pressure caused by a sound (pressure) wave. Simply stated, amplitude describes how much energy a sound wave is carrying as it moves outward from a sound source. Higher amplitude equals higher volume.

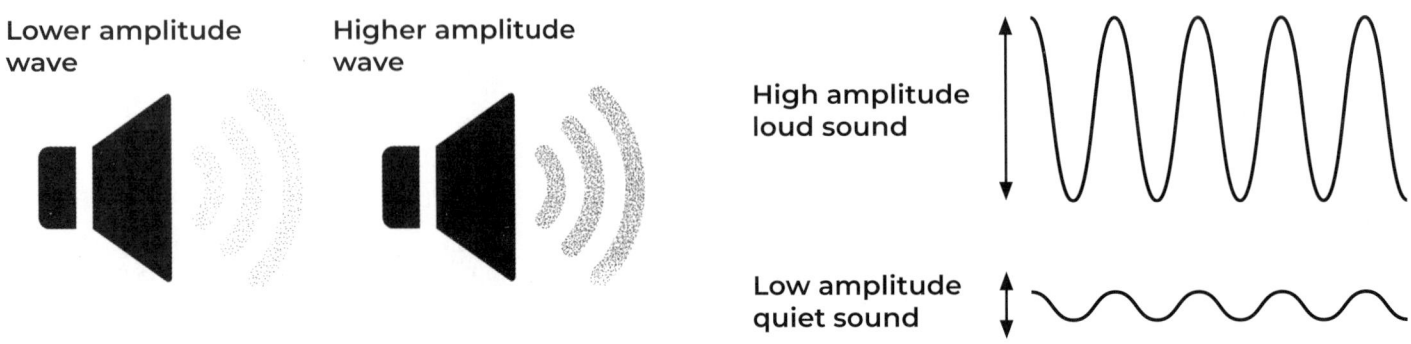

The human ear has an exceptional range of hearing. It can hear fine detail close up, loud noises from a distance, and it also has a mechanism that reduces sensitivity as sound levels increase. The ear does not perceive all frequencies the same way; it is less sensitive to low frequencies and extremely high frequencies. To measure this wide and dynamic range of hearing, we use the decibel scale (dB), which is logarithmic, meaning it increases exponentially, not linearly. This means that on the decibel scale, levels go up in powers of 10. For example, if we are at almost total silence (0 dB), sound energy that is 10 times the intensity is 10 dB, and sound energy that is 100 times the intensity is 20 dB.

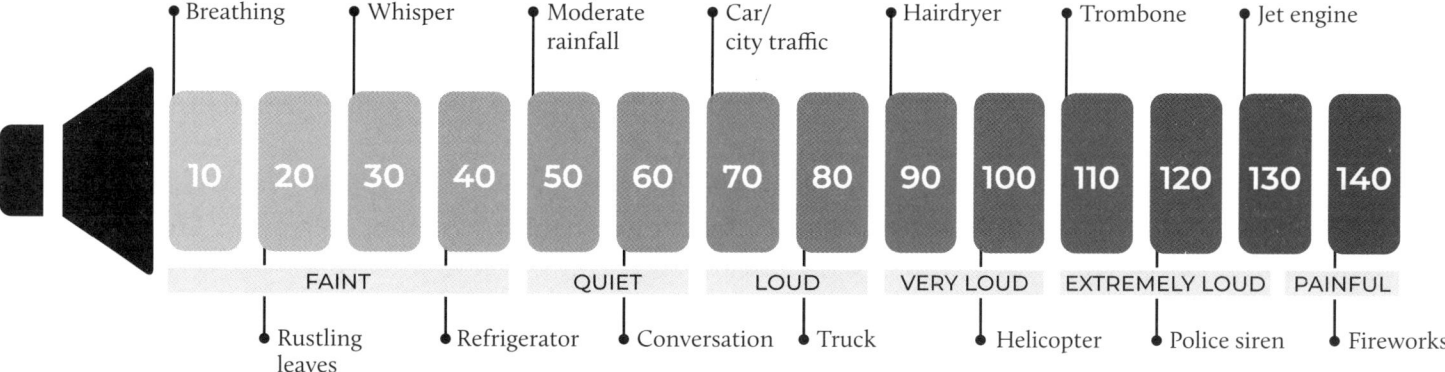

LIMITATIONS

> *"The more you know, the more you know you don't know."*—Aristotle

We use music theory to catalog and explain familiar musical concepts. It is limiting from the perspective of expression because it requires a musician to communicate what is on paper. However, a musician has to interpret a scale or a set of chord changes and make music from it.

Imagine a scenario: You are on a gig and a song that you don't know how to play gets called. The band leader hands you a chart. How you perform the song is based on many factors:

- Have you heard the song before?
- Is it familiar?
- Can you hear other band members well enough to follow by ear?

Let's say you are not at all familiar with the song. The chart (or map) might be all you need to perform the song easily, or it might be confusing and you have to feel your way through it. Limitations arise based on understanding and the ability to express oneself at any given moment. It all comes down to each person's subjective interpretation of the information given.

If you're reading a book and come across an unfamiliar word, you can either look it up or assume the meaning based on how it's used in context. The story is still the story—it is the reader who misses out on the story's depth if too many words are glossed over. Misunderstandings occur all the time due to a word's assumed meaning. Consider the statement "I study jazz." That simple statement can be interpreted very differently based on an individual's background, experience, and age. "Jazz" might be interpreted much differently by a professional jazz musician than by a beginner in the style, a progressive rock musician, or a bluegrass musician. The word "study" could mean a once-a-week lesson or a daily routine. Terms used in music theory can be interpreted differently according to a person's experience and depth of knowledge.

The limitation of language is not often talked about because we have the awareness only of what we as individuals subjectively know. We forget that our assumptions about an experience or thing are our own subjective experience, yet for someone else, the depth of knowledge may far exceed or be far less than our own. Often, the limitation is our own misunderstanding. When playing music, it is good to remember theory and language can be helpful tools to describe what's going on, but it is your responsibility to listen to, interpret, and act on the information given.

CHAPTER 2:
Listening

RELATIONSHIPS

The word "relationship" is often used when describing a connection between people. It's the way in which two or more concepts, objects, or people are connected, or the state of being is connected. If we focus on ourselves as individuals, we'll notice we have relationships with our body, our senses, our mind, and our emotions. We rarely take time to notice the multiple parts that make up the person we are. All those parts are always in a relationship within us. If the mind is in a spin of excessive thoughts, our focus becomes lost in the mind. In that scenario, can we really *hear* at the deepest level we are capable of? A popular quote sums this up in every way: "Energy flows where attention goes." Whatever our attention is focused on, our energy will go there as well. Focus on a problem, and our mind, emotions, and actions get lost in that problem. Focus on learning and understanding, and our mind, emotions, and actions follow the road to discovery.

With ear training, we are cultivating a relationship with listening and hearing at a deeper level than we may have ever reached before. We will identify relationships and subtleties among sound *timbres* (tone qualities) and pitches, and we will make maps of those relationships so we can call them forth at will. With time, patience, and practice, our relationship with hearing will change in the ways we cultivate it with the aid of this book.

ACTIVE LISTENING

Active listening is focused listening. To listen actively is to give one's attention to a sound. Arguably the most important skill in music, and ear training in particular, is the ability to listen. Is listening a skill? Can we get better at it? Indeed, we can!

Can you listen to your friend tell the story of their vacation when you are thinking about what you need to buy at the grocery store on your way home from work? No, you can't. If your mind is in relationship to other thoughts, paying attention to what's in front of you is almost impossible. For most people, thoughts are images in the mind, and these images are running nonstop. To listen fully, you must stop thinking, bring yourself to the present moment, and get in touch with your senses.

Breathing/Listening Exercise

We are going to practice being present and active listening. Remove all potential distractions in your immediate location, sit in a comfortable position, and follow the steps below:

1. Breathe in for a slow count of 5, hold the breath for 8, then release the breath slowly for a count of 10. Focus on your breath and repeat the sequence 5 times.
2. Continue breathing comfortably and begin to focus your attention on any sounds you might hear in your environment.
3. Just notice sound. Do you hear anything? Listen carefully.
4. Pick a sound and see if you can describe it to yourself. Is it a hum, a soft tone, does it rise or fall? Is it rhythmic in nature?
5. See how long you can sit and listen before your mind starts to take over with a thought. Maybe you find your mind wanting to plan something for the future? Or maybe you make a judgment about sitting? Notice whether you're in a hurry to move on. Just notice.
6. Stop.

This exercise is a practice in taking time to listen. Using breath to slow yourself down and bring your attention to the sounds in your surroundings. When you can bring your attention to listening only, you're active listening.

TIMBRE, COLOR, AND NOISE

Another component of sound is *timbre*, which is the color, texture, or quality of a tone. Several different instruments could play the same pitch but sound distinctly different; instruments like the piano, bass, and saxophone all have different sound textures (timbres). Vowels in language have their own unique sounds: A, E, I, O, and U can all be sung at the same pitch but are different enough to recognize.

Another element of sound is noise that doesn't have pitch but is recognizable. The sounds of plucking, hammering, or scraping a string can be compared to consonants in language. Use the consonant T with the vowel sound E and it creates a different sound than the consonant K would when used with the vowel E. The difference is very clear when one is playing a stringed instrument with a pick versus hammering the string.

Why is this important? Hearing tone (pitch) and timbre (color) helps when you are trying to solve the mystery of music. This is a book on training yourself to notice all the nuances of sound.

Timbre, Color, and Noise Exercise

Let's explore timbre and other nuances associated with sound. The same pattern will be played by ten different sampled pianos. Take the time to compare—make listening and noticing a priority. Approach this with as much curiosity as you can. If you desire a career in music as a musician or a sound engineer, this skill is essential.

 TRACK 2 Piano Timbres

1. What kind of piano is this? Can you tell whether it's an upright or a grand?
2. Is it big, small, warm, or brittle sounding? What are the main characteristics of its sound if you had to describe them?
3. Do you hear the room sound? Was the piano recorded in a large, medium, or small room? Can you tell if reverb is used, and if so, what kind of reverb?
4. Does it sound like the microphones were close to the piano or far from it during the recording? Hint: Imagine the microphone is your ear. Are you close to the piano sound or far from it?
5. Notice anything else?
6. Download a list of the pianos used in this exercise.

 Timbre Color Pianos

DYNAMICS

When we train our ears, we are training ourselves to listen to *all* aspects of music. *Dynamics* are the varying levels of volume in different parts of a musical performance. "Depth" is a term that can be used to describe dynamics. As a musician, the ability to respond by listening is critical—first by noticing dynamics, then by matching dynamics. If you are transcribing or mimicking a musical passage from another musician, you have to not only hear the pitch and notice the timbre, but you also have to discern the differences in volume between the notes and phrases. Dynamics are generally used to distinguish certain sections in songs, like when a chorus is louder than a verse. More subtle dynamics between notes create an impact on feel and expression. The best way to explain the more subtle use of dynamics is to give you an example. I played a bass line along with a hi-hat cymbal; both will be played evenly with no fluctuation in dynamics. I'll follow that example with the same parts played with dynamics.

 TRACK 3 Dynamic Example 1, No Dynamics

 TRACK 4 Dynamic Example 2, with Dynamics

Can you hear the difference? Both examples sound fine, but the one with dynamics has more groove. Music is a natural thing like breathing and speaking. We use dynamics in the way we walk, talk, and move around in life.

PART LISTENING

Listening to the relationships among the instruments in a band is another great way to train your ears. "Picking out parts" is what I call it. It is the ability to focus your attention on a single instrument part being played in a song. While it is natural to focus on the instrument you play, what about the other instruments? Can you listen and discern the role each instrument plays to make up the whole song? Transcribers, mixing engineers, and producers are trained to zoom in and out on each part to create the whole. It is an essential listening skill for those careers.

Part Exercise

Think of this exercise as research. Commit yourself to putting in the time, to really dig in and do it right. Follow the steps below:

1. Find a quiet space and remove possible distractions. It might be best to listen with headphones.
2. Pick a song and get out your notebook.
3. Listen to the whole song multiple times with an attention to detail. Analyze everything that's going on. Notice the tempo, harmony, sounds, textures, lyrics, melody, groove, and feel or vibe.
4. Pick out all of the instruments. What's the instrumentation?
5. Pick a specific instrument to focus on. Is it repetitive? Is it playing long or short tones? What is its character? Is it abrasive or soft? Does it mimic a sound in our environment, like a machine or something from nature? What mood is it trying to convey? How does it make you feel?
6. Notice how the musicians and instruments work together to make up the whole.

When you can pick out the parts that make up the whole, listening can be a different experience. The ability to notice subtle variations in time, rhythmic connection, space, duration, pitch, timbre, and dynamics adds more depth to the listening experience. Part listening also translates to live performance. It's important to take any listening experience and experiment with it in different situations. *How* we hear and *what* we hear has everything to do with the amount of focus we put into listening.

LISTENING TO OTHERS

Listening to others is an essential skill in any live performance. How we interact and respond to other musicians in the moment makes the live experience second to none. As a musician matures, focus can shift from individual to band. This is also true with listening. As your overall skill increases, the focus that was once required for your performance can now be placed on listening to and engaging with the band. Listening for pitch, harmony, rhythm, space, and dynamics enter the equation.

LISTEN WHEN YOU PRACTICE

Music is a listening experience, but the process of learning music is also physical and mental. When we work on physical technique, our focus can go 100% into the technical aspect and this is normal. If you play a stringed instrument, finger warm-ups are commonplace. It is good to remind oneself to always bring "listening" back into focus when working on technique. Integrate the movement of your fingers with how that particular movement sounds.

The same is true with understanding music theory; our focus can be on understanding certain concepts versus how those concepts sound in the context of a song. Again, it is good to remind yourself to bring "listening" into whatever you are trying to learn about. For example, you can notice a ii-V-I chord progression written on a lead sheet, but can you hear that ii-V-I chord progression when listening?

An odd thing about music, a major triad can be theoretically understood and physically played, but not recognized and decoded by the ear. This is why we practice ear training, to make that connection.

Timbre Color Pianos

1. **(00:01) Grand Piano** – Clear highs, warm, deep low end. Medium studio sound, no reverb added. Microphones sound close and in the room. I hear detail and the slight room sound.

2. **(00:13) Grand Piano** – Bright highs, deep bass with less mid-range. Concert hall, large hall reverb added. Microphones sound close and distant.

3. **(00:25) Grand Piano** – Mid-range boost and boxy sounding. Small room, no reverb added. Microphones sound close.

4. **(00:37) Grand Piano** – High end isn't as crisp. Low mid-range boost but not boxy. Medium room, no reverb added. Microphones sound close.

5. **(00:49) Grand Piano (Art Deco Piano)** – Clear and full sound, but dark tone. Small room, no reverb added. Microphones sound close.

6. **(01:01) Baby Grand** – Very bright and lacking deep low end. Small room, no reverb added. Microphones sound close.

7. **(01:13) Electric Grand** – Flat, soft attack, less resonant than a real piano. No reverb added. A simulation of a real piano.

8. **(01:25) Upright Piano** – Notes resonate shorter, almost cut off early. Strong mid-range, has the upright "saloon" sound. Small room sound, no reverb added. Microphones sound close.

9. **(01:37) Upright Piano** – Warm, full upright tone. Low notes stick out and I notice the attack of the keys in the stereo field. Medium room, no reverb added. Microphones sound close over the lid.

10. **(01:49) Grand Piano** – Big, deep and washy sounding. Concert hall, large hall reverb added with delay. Microphones sound distant.

CHAPTER 3:
Practice and Motivation

PRACTICE = PERFORMANCE + PROBLEM-SOLVING

Practice is the repeated performance of an activity or skill to acquire and maintain proficiency. For a musician, it's an activity one hopes to carry out on a regular basis and make a habit, a daily routine. This next chapter is about practice and motivation.

Performance

Over the years, one thing I've noticed about exceptional musicians is that they have a love for playing. Many see practice as an opportunity to play music. I frequently ask musicians that I admire about their practice and performance habits. The great ones jam when they practice. Think about it—if you want to get better at expression, you have to do it. To integrate any idea, you must put it to use. Like learning a new word, it doesn't become part of your vocabulary by thinking about it—you have to start using it in sentences when you speak. Actors rehearse lines aloud; musicians rehearse content by performance.

Problem-Solving

Problem-solving is one of the most important skills in life and in a practice routine. See a problem or limitation and find a solution. In music, a problem can be:

- Emotional—not able to express
- Technical—not able to execute
- Mental—not able to comprehend

The issues above are problems that can be solved, but all of them require time and action ... massive action.

A big part of any do-it-yourself project is action, the art of doing something. This chapter explores the mental game of practice, how to stay present, interested, and motivated ... and how to generate action. If action is a struggle for you, there are many books about practice and motivation that can help you; the world is full of guidance. If you are having a problem with any aspect of music or life, you can find a solution by problem-solving the issue.

TALENT

Dr. Carol Dweck, a leading researcher on motivation and author of the book *Mindset*, discusses at length the impact an individual's beliefs about themselves and their abilities have on their performance and ultimate success. Dweck examines two very different approaches to belief in self and learning and the impact they have on performance outcomes. She calls these two approaches *fixed mindset* and *growth mindset*. You may resonate with both mindsets at different places and times in your life, depending upon the task, intrinsic motivation, and other factors. However, after close examination, you'll most likely find that *one* of these mindsets colors and shapes your learning—and motivation to learn—more than the other does.

People with a fixed mindset can believe they are naturally talented, and the internal desire is to keep that belief real. They tend to avoid challenges that might make them look bad. They can give up quickly on difficult challenges. They are critical of others and find the success of others threatening. They don't take feedback well. The main motivation for a fixed-minded person is to look good to themselves and others.

People with a growth mindset believe that no matter what level they are at, they can always improve. These people embrace challenges and understand that life is all about growth. They realize that hard work pays off. They learn from feedback (and actually welcome it) and are inspired by the success of others. The main motivation for a growth-minded person is curiosity.

When I discovered the book *Mindset* in my thirties, I realized I was operating from a fixed mindset more so than I had thought. Practice was an uncomfortable reminder of the holes in my game. I would practice the things I excelled in and avoid what needed work. It was embarrassing to admit, but I had turned down gigs and avoided many learning opportunities—all because I didn't want to feel or look bad. Studies show that your mindset impacts your willingness to practice. This was indeed true for me.

Ear training is hard work; it can be tedious, repetitive, fun, and rewarding.

> *"In a growth mindset, challenges are exciting rather than threatening. So rather than thinking, oh, I'm going to reveal my weakness, you say, wow, here's a chance to grow."*—Carol Dweck

KNOW THYSELF

> *"Knowing yourself is the beginning of all wisdom."*—Aristotle

Self-discovery and personal awareness are critical components to understanding what motivates you to learn. One size does not fit all! Why does a music teacher inspire and motivate one student, while another student feels like that teacher doesn't speak their language? The same is true with a book. It's not the teacher or the author, it is the individual. We speak and learn through our personality types and preferences. Different methods of classifying personality—like the Myers-Briggs test (which identifies 16 personality types), the Enneagram (which has 9 types), and Gardner's 8 types of intelligence—all have categories that narrow down personality and traits in the attempt to better understand how people operate. By knowing the gifts and struggles of your personality, you are better able to achieve a goal or work with other people.

Some musicians are more logical, and theory may intrigue and motivate them to practice. Others who are more physical may have great grooves. They feel music in their bodies and it makes them want to dance. Still, others may be great lyricists because they have greater emotional intelligence and are able to articulate how they feel. We could break down any personality test and see how it relates to musicians we all know, including ourselves. This also makes sense as to why musicians resonate with different styles of music. A study at Heriot-Watt University looked at music and character and found distinct similarities between personality and musical preference.

Let's break musical talent/preference down into five categories to help you identify what you resonate with.

1. **Technical:** The ability to play an instrument technically. The more proficient you are at technique, the more freely you can express your musical ideas without limitations. Examples: warm-up exercises, arpeggios, and any material that challenges technical proficiency.

2. **Mental:** The ability to understand notes, scales, theory, and musical concepts. The more you understand mentally, the easier it is to communicate musical ideas and solve musical problems. Examples: spelling chords, key signatures, and general theory and music concepts. Mental practice can be done without an instrument.

3. **Auditory:** The ability to hear and understand what is heard. This is commonly referred to as having a "good ear." This might include hearing intervals and chord changes, and being able to translate what you hear by transcribing it. Trained auditory skill enables you to recognize patterns by ear and then play those patterns. Examples: ear training, learning songs by ear, and transcription.

4. **Rhythmic:** The ability to "feel" music and groove. Having a sense of time and being able to embody a pulse. Examples: sight reading, subdivision, and timing practice.

5. **Creative:** Expressing oneself using music. Developing ideas when improvising or creating parts and melodies when writing music. Examples: composition, improvisation, and musical playing.

I use the words "talent" and "preference" to imply that, with time and focus, what now appears as a talent (therefore a preference) may change as you evolve. Developing relationships with all these areas will help you become the musician you are looking to be.

Know Thyself

Rate yourself on the following categories.

1. **Technical:** The ability to play an instrument technically. The more proficient you are at technique, the more freely you are able to express your musical ideas without limitations. Examples: warm up exercises, arpeggios, and material that challenges technical proficiency.
2. **Mental:** The ability to understand notes, scales, theory, and musical concepts. The more you understand mentally, the easier it is to communicate musical ideas and solve musical problems. Examples: spelling chords, key signatures, general theory, and music concepts. Mental practice can be done without an instrument.
3. **Auditory:** The ability to hear and understand what is heard. This is commonly referred to as having a "good ear." This might include hearing intervals and chord changes, and being able to translate what you hear by transcribing it. Trained auditory skill enables you to recognize patterns by ear and then play those patterns. Examples: ear training, learning songs by ear, and transcription.
4. **Rhythmic:** The ability to "feel" music and groove. Having a sense of time and being able to embody a pulse. Examples: sight reading, subdivision, and timing practice.
5. **Creative:** Expressing oneself using music. Developing ideas when improvising or creating parts and melodies when writing music. Examples: composition, improvisation, and musical playing.

CATEGORIES	STRENGTHS? (NUMBER 1-5)	EASIEST? (NUMBER 1-5)
Technical		
Mental		
Auditory		
Rhythmic		
Creative		

What categories do you practice most often? Assign a numerical rank from 1 to 5 to each category, with 1 indicating the highest frequency and 5 indicating the least frequent.

Do you want to improve on different areas of music? If so, are you willing to change your practice routine? Create a new practice routine by reorganizing the frequency, giving priority to the areas that were less frequent in the previous routine.

CATEGORIES	OLD PRACTICE ROUTINE (1-5)	NEW PRACTICE ROUTINE (1-5)
Technical		
Mental		
Auditory		
Rhythmic		
Creative		

Know Thyself Exercise

1. Get out your notebook or download 📄 **Know Thyself**.
2. Which categories are your strengths? List them in order from best to worst. (1 = strongest)
3. Which categories are the easiest (most natural) and most fun for you? List them in order from best to worst.

CATEGORIES	STRENGTHS? (NUMBER 1-5)	EASIEST? (NUMBER 1-5)
Technical		
Mental		
Auditory		
Rhythmic		
Creative		

Question: Are both lists (strengths and easiest) the same, or very similar?

Which categories do you practice most often? Assign a numerical rank from 1 to 5 to each category, with 1 indicating the highest frequency and 5 indicating the least frequent.

CATEGORIES	OLD PRACTICE ROUTINE (1-5)	NEW PRACTICE ROUTINE (1-5)
Technical		
Mental		
Auditory		
Rhythmic		
Creative		

Do you want to improve on different areas of music? If so, are you willing to change your practice routine? Create a new practice routine by reorganizing the frequency, giving priority to the areas that were less frequent in the previous routine.

We often practice and have the most fun with what we're best at. Experiment by practicing the things at the bottom of your list first. Another thing you can do is ask a friend how they would rate you. Identify and embrace what you're good at. Also, look at what doesn't come as easily for you and see if you can step up your passion and practice those areas in a fun way.

CAUSE AND EFFECT

Cause and effect is a relationship between events whereby a cause creates an effect. Life is built on the law of cause and effect, which exists in both the mental and physical realms:

- If you exercise and take care of your body, it responds by performing and looking better.
- If you have a positive outlook on life, you notice positive things. If you believe people are looking to take advantage of you, that is how you will interpret the actions of other people. Inside the brain is a bundle of nerves called the reticular activating system (RAS), which filters out information. The RAS looks for information in the outside world to validate your internal beliefs. If you believe you are dumb, you will find evidence to support that belief.

It's rather simple to understand cause and effect, yet we seem generally disconnected from how much it affects us. Choice is what shapes our life both physically and mentally. Ask yourself, in this moment, am I making a choice that will create a result I'd prefer? That's it! In the moment, learn to be conscious of your choices. You can make it a practice.

With regard to learning—whether by yourself, in a classroom, or in private lessons—if you surrender and give it your best effort, you'll get the most out of the learning process. If you start to resist and make excuses, you'll find that your results mirror your effort.

PATIENCE/MISTAKES

The biggest issue for any learning experience is having patience with yourself. Ear training development can be hard at times, and if making mistakes is something you want to avoid, then you will avoid practicing—which is not what you want!

Failure, or a mistake, is a feedback mechanism that lets you know what to practice. It shows you the areas you can develop in, and that is the most critical component of growth.

How can we welcome mistakes and honor the journey to improvement? Thomas Edison is a great example. He made 1,000 unsuccessful attempts at creating the light bulb before he succeeded.

> *"I didn't fail 1,000 times. The light bulb was an invention with 1,000 steps."*—Thomas Edison

How do you push yourself without letting the pressure of improving get in the way of learning?

> *"A person who never made a mistake never tried anything new."*—Albert Einstein

Practicing with patience is one of the most important ways to develop as a musician. Our desire to learn quickly can sabotage us over time. Learning is a complex process that involves the mind for understanding and the body for execution. When we are in a hurry, mistakes often happen. Our biology can't discern mistakes—a mistake will "imprint" just the same as if we had done something the correct way. New research about myelin in our brains points directly to the importance of learning things slowly. Myelin is a lipid-rich substance that forms slowly to insulate cell axons (paths or wires) in the brain to increase electrical impulses. If you practice slowly and fully understand a concept from the start, the pathways you are forming in the brain for that particular skill are the best ones possible.

GOALS AND HAVING A PLAN

> *"A goal without a plan is just a wish."—Antoine de Saint-Exupéry*

A lack of motivation generally lines up with a lack of a plan or goal. People wish and dream all the time, but a plan takes the wish and makes it tangible; it's a commitment. Maybe that's the scary part for people … having to step out of the wish and make it a reality. I've heard the saying: "People don't tell you what they want—they tell you what they don't want." Knowing what you want takes some reflection. You took action by purchasing this book, which is like buying a map of a city you'd like to go to. Now it's time to decide when and how. That's what a plan is!

If you are going to take a trip, having a clear vision of where you want to go is the first step. Viewing your musical evolution as a journey to be taken is a practical analogy. This perspective helps the intangible, internal world of ideas and emotions evolve into an external experience.

If you have a plan, you can take tangible steps on your trip. You know which way to turn, and if you get lost, you can look at the map and get yourself back on track. If you take a detour, you can get back on track anytime. If you don't have a plan, where do you start? Where are you going?

A goal is the object of a person's ambition or effort. Goals help shape focus, and they can be changed and adapted over time. As life changes, so do we, and so can our goals. Setting goals actively shapes your future and progress; it gives you a vision from which to guide your actions. A goal *pulls* you toward the future; it is fuel for motivation.

GOAL = VISION + ACTION (specific action)

Creating goals can involve a simple short-term step or a more elaborate process that will be described shortly. Be specific about what, when, and how. I have given goal examples as a handout to help you in the process.

 Goal Examples

 Goal Handout (Week, Month, and Quarter)

GOAL EXERCISES

> *"We can only be what we give ourselves the power to be."—Obert Skye*

The following exercise can be used for any kind of goal, big or small. Do it when you have time to imagine and focus on yourself. It involves just you, your notebook or the PDF handout, and a pen or pencil. This exercise is a visualization that is audio only. If you're reading this book, go to the audio version of this exercise.

Simple Goals

A *simple goal* is a goal that is more short-term and single-minded in focus. It orients well with a performance or musical concept that can be measured easily. The future performance helps fuel the goal and the action needed.

 TRACK 5 Simple Goal Visualization

Simple Goal Formula

- **Vision:** What do you want to achieve? Imagine it—picture it in your mind. Write it down. Make it simple and concise.
- **Action:** What action or steps do you need to take to make your vision happen?
- **Timeline:** When will you do it? How often? Be specific. Time(s) and location?
- **Is it realistic?** Don't set yourself up to fail. It's better to exceed your action items than to fall short and stop working toward the goal. For example: Don't say you'll practice for an hour if that's pushing it. Set aside 15 minutes instead. You can always exceed the time allotted.

Major Goals

A *major goal*, or *life goal*, is the "big picture" and relates more to a purpose or meaning. It uses your vision of the life you want as fuel and motivation. It involves how you see your future and what you want your life to be. This is the umbrella for all other goals and is followed by a *long-term goal* (a far-in-the-future hope, something you really want to work toward), a *mid-term goal* (one that is reachable in a year and supports your long-term goal), and a *short-term goal* (one that is attainable within a few months and dictates your current practice routine).

 TRACK 6 Major Goal Visualization

Life Goals Formula

- **Major goal vision:** What do you want for your life? Make it big. If you could have it, what would "it" be? Imagine yourself 10 years in the future—picture it in your mind. Write it down. List it. Make it simple and concise.
- **Long-term goal:** This is a goal for about 5 years in the future, and it supports the major goal.
    - **Vision:** What do you want to achieve that fits under your major goal? Imagine it—picture it in your mind. Write it down. Make it simple and concise.
    - **Action:** What action items can you do now to support your major goal?
    - **Timeline:** When will you do the action(s)? This can be a practice routine that you do twice a month. You don't expect immediate results from this action, but it supports your major goal.
- **Mid-term goal:** This is a goal for about 6 to 12 months in the future, and it supports your long-term goal.
    - **Vision:** What can you achieve within a year that supports your long-term goal? Imagine it.
    - **Action:** What action items can you do now to support your long-term goal?
    - **Timeline:** How often does it require action to be achieved in a year? When will you do it? Be specific. Time(s) and location? Is it realistic? Don't set yourself up to fail. It's better to exceed your action items than to fall short and stop working toward the goal.

Short-term goal: This is a goal for about 1 to 4 months in the future.
- **Vision:** What can you achieve within a few months that supports your goal? Imagine it.
- **Action:** What action items can you do now to attain that goal?
- **Timeline:** When will you work on it? How often? Be specific. Time(s) and location? Is it realistic?

You can have several goals in each area of music, or a few smaller goals under a major goal. For some people, articulating what they want for themselves creates passion for life and music. What we are trying to do is pull you toward your future. Knowing where you want to go and putting it in writing makes a world of difference.

HABITS

> *"We are what we repeatedly do. Excellence, then, is not an act, but a habit."*—Aristotle

What we do in our daily routine sets the course of our lives. Humans are habitual creatures. Modifying a routine takes awareness and thought followed by action. We often want something new without a plan. I want to practice more … I want to lose weight … but without specifics, the plan falls short.

Specifics, you ask? The action (what) and the time (when)—it's that simple!

So, if the process of achieving goals is simple, why does it so often elude us? Lack of action. We like to visualize ourselves at the happy ending when our goals and dreams are realized. A habit is an action, something you routinely do. If you are curious and willing to add practice routines to your day, they become part of your life. In time, these actions become something you crave. Some days you may not feel like practicing; this is a common problem. Steven Pressfield calls this problem "resistance" in his book *The War of Art*. It's this initial resistance that one must step through. Often, just starting an activity sets everything in motion.

Replace

A good way to create a new habit is to replace a habit that you *don't* want with a new habit.

Example: Every morning, I used to get up and look online at used bass guitars when I drank my coffee. I replaced that time, which was about 15 minutes, with a sight-reading practice. I now look forward to my morning coffee and sight-reading. The feeling of accomplishment far exceeds the pleasure of looking at cool basses that I'm not going to buy!

Add On

Another great way to add a habit is by doing the new habit right after or before a current habit. In your mind, you will associate the new habit with the habit that is already established.

Example: I get up from my desk several times a day and refill my water. It's a regular habit. I added push-ups after I put my water down. Now when I work, I get several sets of push-ups in throughout the day, which is good for me, and it doesn't take much time.

Habit Exercise

Replacing and adding onto a habit have both a "what" and a "when"—an action and a time.

1. Get your notebook out and list your habits or regular activities.
    a. What habits or rituals do you do in the morning?
    b. What habits or rituals do you do in the afternoon?
    c. What habits or rituals do you do in the evening?

2. Do you have a habit (or habits) you would like to replace? Write it down.
    a. How much time does it take?
    b. What would you replace it with?

3. Do you have any current habits or activities before or after which you could add a new one?
    a. What could you add?
    b. How much time are you willing to spend?
    c. Suggestion: Pick a new interval each week and practice it for five minutes after a regular daily activity two times a day. It's the small things that add up when it comes to practice.

> *"Depending on what they are, our habits will either make us or break us. We become what we repeatedly do."—Steven Covey*

OPTIMIZE

> *"You are the average of the five people you spend the most time with."—Jim Rohn*

The people you spend time with, your physical environment, and what you focus your attention on has everything to do with the person you are and the person you will most likely become.

What is your environment like? Is it conducive to the life you want? Does it support your goals?

Let's look at a few things that can optimize your outcome.

Distractions

Technology can help in so many great ways, but it can also be the biggest obstacle to our development. Why? Distraction. Put objects or devices in a different location or turn off all sounds and notifications while practicing. If possible, use a different device for practice that isn't tied to social media. You can find several studies online about distractions due to technology and student focus lasting only between 3 and 6 minutes! A 20-minute practice can turn into a 4-minute scattered activity if the phone keeps you from focusing. If you want to stay on track, keep distractions, temptations, and all things that could get in your way ... *out* of the way.

Symbols and Inspiration

A symbol is an object that represents or stands for something, like when a physical object represents something internal. Surround yourself with inspirational images, objects, and quotes. This is especially helpful in your practice space.

Easy Access

Make sure that the tools you need are easily available in your environment. Keep instruments out of their cases and set up so you can grab them for a quick 5-minute ear training session.

Watch and Visualize

The first stage of learning is imitation. From birth on, we have carefully observed our parents and caregivers in order to learn, to form words with our mouths, and to express emotions with our faces. Our brains fire off a subset of the same neurons when we are watching someone do something we are familiar with. What does that mean? It means that watching a musician play, in essence, is a form of practice. Watching and being in the energy of a live performance is palpable; it's something you can feel and use as motivation. Similarly, visualization is also useful for intermediate and advanced players. Make the time to have fun when listening; stop and connect to the music.

PRACTICE LOG

A practice log is a great way to maintain the integrity of your goals. Write down what you intend to work on each week or each time you practice. When the time comes to practice, go through each item on your list—or a few of the items, depending on your available time. Generally, the most effective way to practice is to apply short bursts of focus in several different areas. Tackle challenging items on your list when you're most focused—this is usually early in the practice session. Practice is a time to problem-solve any issues you're having. Areas of practice are:

- Technical
- Mental
- Auditory
- Rhythmic
- Creative
- Repertoire

Review your **Know Thyself Exercise** and your goals when making a practice log. Building a catalog of music for performance is called repertoire. If you have a performance in the future, add material for that as well.

A practice log is a way to organize your thoughts and follow up with yourself at the end of the day or week. Be sure to download the Practice Log PDF. A practice log example PDF is also available to help with ideas.

 Practice Log

 Practice Log Examples

PRACTICE TYPE	Item List (Be specific)	Sun	Mon	Tue	Wed	Thur	Fri	Sat
MENTAL *(Theory & practice without instrument)*	1							
	2							
	3							
AUDITORY *(Ear training)*	1							
	2							
	3							
RHYTHMIC *(Timing, feel & sight reading)*	1							
	2							
	3							
TECHNICAL *(Chops, rudiments & skills)*	1							
	2							
	3							
CREATIVE *(Playing, performance & composition)*	1							
	2							
	3							
REPERTOIRE *(Personal music & business)*	1							
	2							
	3							

CHAPTER 4:
Understanding Intervals

INTERVALS

As mentioned previously, an interval is the distance between two pitches or notes. Chords and scales are built from intervals. When you listen to music, what you are hearing is an interplay of intervals.

HALF STEP AND WHOLE STEP

In music, half steps and whole steps are the smallest intervals or distances between two consecutive pitches. A *half step*, also known as a *semitone*, is the smallest interval in Western music. It is the distance between two frets on a guitar or two adjacent keys on a piano. A *whole step*, also known as a *whole tone*, is twice the distance of a half step. Two half steps equal a whole step. Understanding the concept of half steps and whole steps is essential for understanding scales.

SCALES

Western music is built using 12-tone *equal temperament*. The frequency between each of these tones has the same ratio, meaning the distance between each tone is the same. A musical *scale* is an organized sequence of notes. The *chromatic scale* is built using all 12 notes available. The *diatonic scales* have 7 notes, and these are what keys are based on. We will be using the major scale and the minor scale to help explain all the different intervals. Different scales, such as major and minor, follow specific patterns of whole and half steps. By manipulating these intervals, musicians can create different sounds in their compositions.

KEYS

A musical *key* is a tonal system based on a major or minor scale and the chords derived from it. Like a scale, a key gets its name from the first note or *tonic*. A *key signature* appears at the beginning of a piece of music to tell us the key and which notes will be *sharp* (♯) or *flat* (♭) throughout. (A sharp raises a note a half step. A flat lowers a note a half step.)

INTERVALS 101

We will use the key of C (which has no sharps or flats) for all examples unless indicated. Below is the C *major scale* with the notes labeled. You can refer to each note of the major scale with *scale degrees*: the numbers 1–2–3–4–5–6–7–8, with 1 being the tonic and 8 being the octave of the tonic.

To identify intervals on a musical staff, count the lines and spaces between two notes and *include* the line or space that each note is on C(1), D(2), E(3), F(4), etc.

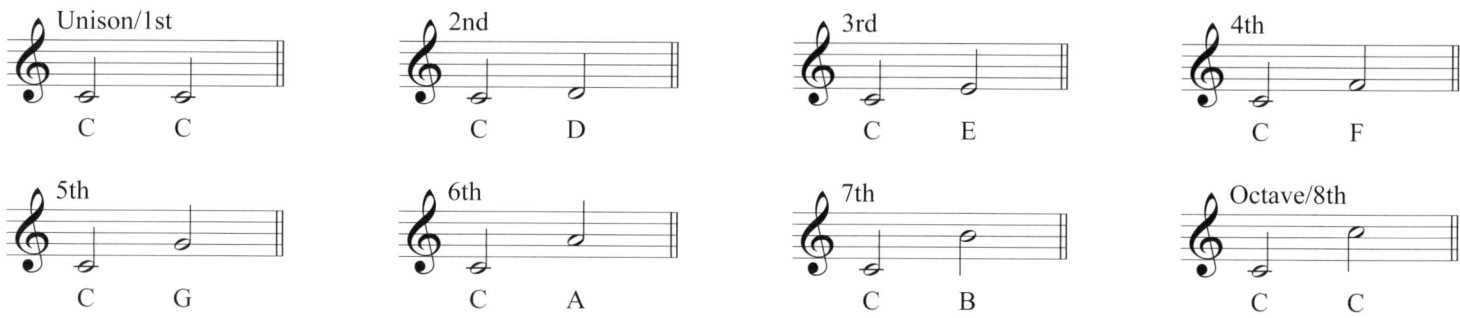

An interval that is measured from the lower note to the higher note (going up) is an *ascending interval*. An interval measured from the higher note to the lower note (going down) is a *descending interval*.

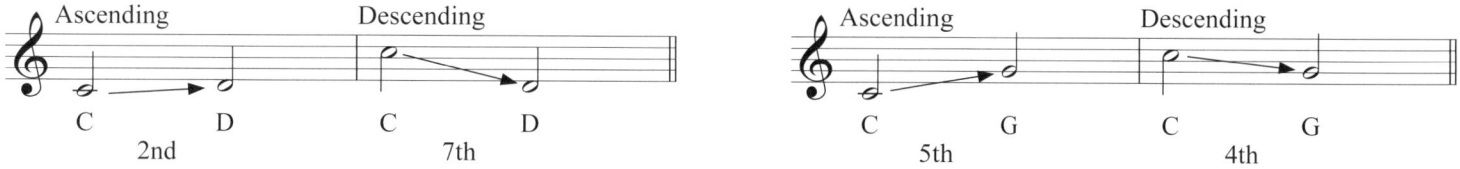

We are only measuring distance in the examples above. The 8th, or octave, is still the tonic, but the distance descending is different from the distance ascending. When referring to the intervals in a key, they are counted with the letters in ascending order. For example, in the key of C, F is scale degree 4. From the octave, C down to F is a 5th in distance, but F is still scale degree 4.

ASCENDING AND DESCENDING SOUNDS

Because measuring the distance is different for ascending and descending intervals, we must learn these sounds from the tonic of the scale *up* and from the octave of the tonic *down*. This creates 13 different sounds to identify in each direction. Focusing on the ascending sounds first will help build associations that can be used with the descending sounds. Descending interval practice is covered in Chapter 8.

PERFECT INTERVALS

The unison (1st), 4th, 5th, and octave (8th) are *perfect intervals*. Perfect intervals have a pure, hollow sound and are the same whether in a major scale or in a minor scale—hence the name "perfect."

MAJOR AND MINOR INTERVALS

The 2nd, 3rd, 6th, and 7th can be either major or minor, depending on the scale or key.

Major Scale

Let's look at every interval of the major scale. In the example below, the tonic note (C) is shown below each scale tone to clearly demonstrate each interval.

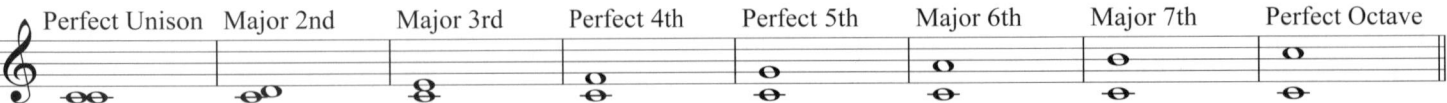

Minor Scale

When we lower a major interval by a half step, it creates a minor interval. When you lower the 3rd, 6th, and 7th of a major scale by a half step, you get the *natural minor scale*.

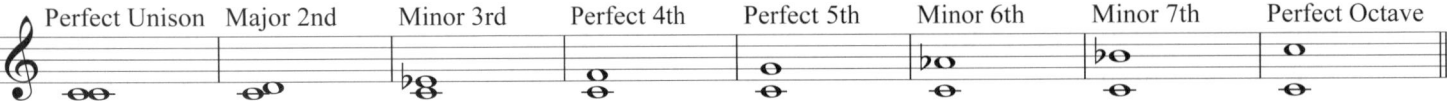

Some minor scales have a minor 2nd instead of a major 2nd. Drop the major 2nd a half step to create a minor 2nd. (More on this in Chapter 7.)

AUGMENTED AND DIMINISHED

When a 4th or 5th is raised a half step, the result is an *augmented* interval. When a 4th or 5th is lowered a half step, the result is a *diminished* interval. A diminished 5th is also called a *tritone* ("tri" meaning three—in this case, three whole steps from the tonic).

Both terms are most often used when modifying a perfect 5th. However, augmented 4ths are usually referred to as raised or sharpened 4ths. You may notice this creates multiple names for some intervals. Why? When using theory to describe what's going on in a particular song or musical idea, intervals have different functions, especially in chords. Having different names helps to describe a particular interval function in a specific key.

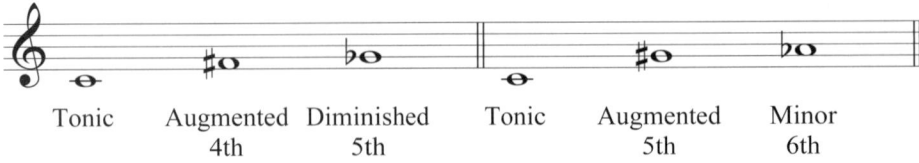

COMPOUND INTERVALS

All intervals within the range of one octave are *simple intervals*. When an interval is larger than an octave in distance, it is a *compound interval*. Add the number 7 to a simple interval to get the compound equivalent. For example:

- A 2nd one octave higher is a 9th (2 + 7 = 9).
- A 4th one octave higher is an 11th (4 + 7 = 11).
- A 6th one octave higher is a 13th (6 + 7 = 13).

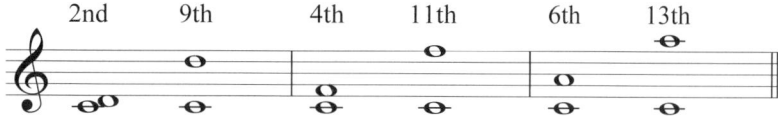

In chord theory, these compound intervals are called *extensions*. Using the compound interval or extension lets one know the location of a particular interval, and this is especially useful when playing chords.

LABELING INTERVALS

Qualities

P = Perfect
M = Major
m = Minor
A or + = Augmented
d, dim, or ° = Diminished

Intervals within an Octave

P1 = Perfect Unison
m2 = Minor 2nd
M2 = Major 2nd
m3 = Minor 3rd
M3 = Major 3rd
P4 = Perfect 4th
A4 = Augmented 4th
d5 = Diminished 5th
P5 = Perfect 5th
m6 = Minor 6th
M6 = Major 6th
m7 = Minor 7th
M7 = Major 7th
P8 = Perfect Octave

MELODIC/MELODY

Pitches or notes played separately, one after the other, are called *melodic intervals*. A *melody* is created by using notes through time to paint a picture or have a conversation. How those notes interact with one another in sound, distance, and rhythm creates a feeling much like a story can, with a rising and falling or a surprise leap into the unknown. We've all heard melodies that play over and over in our minds, either from a song or commercial.

HARMONIC/HARMONY

Pitches played simultaneously are called *harmonic intervals*. These are the building blocks of chord structure and *harmony* in a piece of music. The harmony of a song is like the backdrop or setting for a melody. Two notes played simultaneously is a *double stop*, while three or more notes played at the same time is a *chord*.

CONSONANT AND DISSONANT

The word *consonant* means to be in agreement, or in harmony. In musical terms, consonant refers to intervals that sound stable, pleasing, or resolved.

The 3rd and 6th are consonant intervals. If you play them melodically or harmonically, they sound stable and can stand on their own. I'll play some examples of consonant intervals. Focus your attention and listen.

 TRACK 7 Consonant Samples

Notice the harmonic stability and pleasing sounds of the intervals. What do you hear? It's important to articulate your own sense of these sounds.

The word *dissonant* means clashing, lacking in harmony, or unusual in combination. Dissonant intervals sound unstable and create unrest. Why might you want to use a dissonant interval? Music reflects life, and life is full of unrest moving toward rest. When things are uncomfortable, we tend to move forward until they are comfortable again. The tension created by dissonance creates interest, movement, and resolution.

The 2nd and 7th are dissonant intervals. Here are some examples of dissonant intervals.

 TRACK 8 Dissonant Samples

Notice the unease in the sounds. What do you hear?

INTERVAL CHARACTERISTICS

> *"You can know the name of a bird in all the languages of the world, but when you're finished, you'll know absolutely nothing whatever about the bird. So let's look at the bird and see what it's doing—that's what counts. I learned very early the difference between knowing the name of something and knowing something."*
> —Richard Feynman

Train your ears to know the uniqueness of each interval. Here are two things to consider when trying to break down a sound:

- **Character:** Each interval has an inherent quality that the two notes create when they come together. Here are some questions you can ask when trying to define the sound:
    › Is it consonant or dissonant?
    › Do the notes of the interval clash or do they resonate?
    › How do *you* hear the interval? Does it have a particular aspect or quality that distinguishes it from other intervals?
- **Distance:** The distance, or size, of an interval is the relationship of a note to the tonic or octave. A large melodic distance can create energy and excitement in a phrase, while a small span can create subtle movement. The size of an interval is a characteristic that can be very easy for your ear to recognize, especially the larger ones.

When you want to understand a concept, it requires study and time. Identifying details and having a consistent relationship to what you are learning enables the information to become part of you. It stores on your human hard drive just like all the other information you now know.

SOLFÈGE

Solfège is a system that assigns syllables to scale tones to teach pitch relationships and sight singing. We use these syllables to *audiate* the music in front of us. (To audiate basically means to think musically.) Using solfège for ear training is not necessary, but it can be worth your time if it's something you'd like to explore. You can substitute or add solfège syllables to the scale degrees or interval names. The two types of solfège are *fixed "do"* and *movable "do"* ("do" is pronounced like "doe," a deer).

Movable "Do"

In the movable "do" system, the syllables are tied to scale degrees. "Do" is always the 1st degree of the major scale, regardless of the key. Movable "do" is used more often than fixed "do" due to its key-centered approach in which one can hear the intervals of the scale as they function within the key. Movable "do" is best used for relative pitch.

Fixed "Do"

In the fixed "do" system, the syllables are always tied to the same pitches. For instance, "do" corresponds to a specific note, C. If we were in the key of D, we would start on the syllable "re." Fixed "do" is preferable for more complex or difficult tonality. It is also the preferred system for perfect pitch.

Chromatic Solfège Scale

In the following chart, the middle row shows the syllables for the major scale tones, the top row shows the syllables for the ascending (or sharp) tones, and the bottom row shows the syllables for the descending (or flat) tones.

Ascending (sharp) tones	→	di		ri			fi		si		li			di		→
Major scale tones		do		re		mi		fa		sol		la		ti		do		re
Descending (flat) tones	←		ra		me				se		le		te			ra	←

CHAPTER 5:
Ear Training Template

Since this is a do-it-yourself book, I expect you'll adapt the following information to an approach that works best for you. The idea is to explore and create different ways of practicing. Below, we break down ear training into a seven-step template. Doing all seven is a very thorough approach. It's good to work with a few of the steps and integrate them into your practice routine. I'll explain each step in detail to help you learn and create your own templates for future self-discovery.

SEVEN-STEP EAR TRAINING TEMPLATE

1. Listening Exercise
2. Mimic Exercise
3. Melodic Exercise
4. Harmonic Exercise
5. Visualization Exercise
6. Meditation Exercise
7. Composition Exercise

IDENTIFY

The first step in ear training is the ability to identify what we hear. Theory is an important step in the process because we need to label what we are hearing. We identify a sound and then use theory to classify and categorize it. This process is used for intervals, rhythms, scales, cadences, chord types, and other melodic and chordal information. The music-making process involves listening (taking music in), internalizing, interpreting, and expressing (letting music out).

1. Listening Exercise

In Chapter 2, we did a listening exercise related to "active listening." It started with breathing, holding your breath, and exhaling. If you forgot how to do this, now is a great time to go back and review. Why? So you can relax and bring your focus to the present moment. State of mind is part and parcel of effective practice. It's more productive to have a few minutes of focused practice than it is to spend an hour easily distracted and in a hurry. Doing an initial listening exercise helps integrate the theoretical information with the sound. Follow these steps:

1. **Set up:** Set up your environment, relax, and prepare to practice and explore. If needed, do the breathing exercise from Chapter 2 to get in the correct state of mind. Remove any potential distractions.
2. **Listen:** Don't play along with an instrument until you listen. Be curious.
3. **Analyze/interpret:** What characteristics do you notice? Are the sounds consonant or dissonant? How much distance or space is there between the notes? What else?
4. **Take notes:** Put your thoughts on paper to solidify them and have them available for review. Thoughts can come and go. If you write them down, there is a better chance of remembering and internalizing them. Write down anything that will help you identify the sound.

The listening process will evolve by trial and error; adjust accordingly. This is a great first step when practicing anything new. Whatever you practice, make active listening part of the process.

ASSOCIATION/REFERENCE

Have you ever tried to remember someone's name by associating them with someone else? This is a very useful trick, especially if you have a hard time remembering names (like I do). For example, I recently bought a house, and to remember my neighbor's names, I used association. His name was John, which was my best friend's name, so that was easy for me to remember. Her name was Adrian, so I associated it with the name of Rocky's wife in the 1976 movie *Rocky*. I laughed to myself, yelling "Adrian" in my head in Rocky's voice, but that made it easy to remember!

You can do the same thing with intervals. A way to help the identification process is by associating familiar songs or passages with intervals, scales, or chords. Find a musical example you can refer to. For instance, the theme from *Jaws* uses two notes that are a half step apart (a minor second). Using a familiar tune—one that you can already hear in your mind—will help you to recognize and recall the associated interval(s). Find your own examples for intervals or anything else you want to hear in your mind's ear. There are several websites with lists of songs that you can associate with particular intervals. Search "reference songs for intervals" or "ear training songs."

Practice Note: Associate a familiar song with the sound of an interval, chord, or scale to help you remember it. Try to notice intervals in parts and melodies.

SINGING

Singing or humming can help you internalize music, and it is a major part of ear training. This is not about becoming a singer—it is about connecting pitches to your internal world. You don't have to sing; you can hum instead if that works for you. It's important to adjust the octaves as needed to accommodate your vocal range. If an exercise feels too high, it's best not to strain your voice. Feel free to lower the octave and continue with the exercise.

If you are uncomfortable with singing at first, find a private space. Remember, this is about learning and using your voice as a measuring stick to hear pitches internally. Once you establish a strong sense of pitch, you can then do it in your mind. The upside to practicing this skill is that you will gain confidence in your ear and become a better singer, which helps in any musical situation. Singing helps to make you a well-rounded musician. Imagine being able to express what you hear in your head to another person. We've become a culture that watches others do, versus doing it ourselves. Luckily, you've bought a book entitled "Do-It-Yourself," which is about finding a practice and making things happen.

2. Mimic Exercise

Mimicking can be done on an instrument, but singing is the best way to imprint a sound internally. With any exercise, engage the voice and use it to internalize what you hear. Sing the parts you play when you jam; sing the melody of a song. When it comes to ear training, singing is your best tool to imprint external sound on the internal mind. (Again, you can hum if you are resistant to singing.)

Mimicking is the most common type of exercise to familiarize yourself with a sound:

1. Play and listen to the notes (intervals, etc.) that you want to study.

2. Mimic the sounds you hear. Sing or hum them back to get them into your mind's ear.

3. State out loud (identify) what you are singing; this could be the interval, the note names, or anything else that pertains to what you want to learn.

We'll use the interval of a 5th. Play, listen, and mimic by singing the notes. Play the tonic (the 1), play the 5, and then sing aloud: "one (or root), five."

 TRACK 9 Mimic Example 1

Or you can do it like this: Play the 5, the 1, the 5, the 1, and then sing aloud: "five, one, five, one." You can replace "one" and "five" with note names if you prefer. The idea is to play and mimic.

 TRACK 10 Mimic Example 2

If the pitches are too high, sing them an octave lower. This exercise can move up in half steps and then go back down.

RECALL/AUDIATION

Recall, the second step of the Mimic Exercise, is the ability to retain what we hear and then reproduce it. *Audiation* is another word for retention and recall.

Audiation is hearing music in your head without hearing it in the real world. Aural imagination. Try singing "You Are My Sunshine" or "Mary Had a Little Lamb" in your mind only. Can you imagine it? Audiation can be described as your "mind's ear" versus your "mind's eye."

Take a few minutes and see whether you can recall and sing anything from memory. How did you do?

As mentioned in a previous section, audiation is the musical version of thinking. Most people think in images; if I tell you to picture an elephant walking in tall grass, an image of an elephant walking in tall grass will arise in your mind's eye.

If you play an instrument, you can most likely play scales and other patterns, but may not actually hear them in your mind. Over time, those patterns become familiar, and you will be able to audiate, or hear them in your mind, due to repetition.

How do you strengthen this skill? Sing or hum along to everything you play. Singing helps strengthen audiation because you are internalizing the music by hearing it with your ears and translating it through the senses into the mind. Picture your brain as the computer and your voice as the audio interface. The ability to hear pitches and rhythms along with different timbres is all audiation.

Understanding music and being able to hear it in your mind's ear can expand your creativity, because you can even think of and compose new music in your head. Transcribing without an instrument is also audiation.

Use audiation to test yourself when practicing. See whether you can call forth melodies or parts from memory like we did with "You Are My Sunshine." With intervals, play a note and sing the interval from memory, then check it on an instrument.

3. Melodic Exercise

This ear training exercise involves audiation. You will hear a tonic note and then sing an interval from memory. Any melodic material can be practiced the same way with slight modification.

1. Play the tonic.
2. Sing the tonic and the interval. This is just like the Mimic Exercise from the previous section, but you are filling in the interval from memory.
3. Check the pitch on your instrument after you sing.

Let's use the 5th again. Play the tonic, then sing the tonic and interval, like this:

 TRACK 11 Melodic Example

In the audio, the answers to all the examples will be played after a short pause, so you can check your pitches right after singing them.

Options:

- Play the top note of the interval and sing the tonic. Instead of always practicing tonic to interval, it's important to change the order and direction.
- You can sing the note names instead of the interval if you'd prefer. Instead of "one, five," you could use the exact pitches. It's a great way to learn the notes on your instrument as well.
- Practice the intervals of a chord melodically. Play the tonic and sing the intervals that are in the chord. You can practice scales and other melodic ideas using this same principal.

4. Harmonic Exercise

This exercise involves hearing notes played at the same time, like a double stop or chord. The goal is to hear each pitch separately and sing it. This is a great exercise for practicing triads and other types of chords.

1. Play the interval harmonically (at the same time).
2. Sing the tonic and the interval.
3. Check each interval after you sing.

Again, we'll use the 5th. Play the tonic and interval harmonically, sing the intervals, like this:

 TRACK 12 **Harmonic Example**

Play the tonic and 5th, then sing aloud "one" (check pitch against the audio) and sing aloud "five" (check pitch against audio). For the examples, the chord will be held. Then after a short pause, the tonic will be played. After another short pause, the interval will be played melodically.

Options:

- Sing the interval first. Instead of always practicing tonic to interval, it's important to change the order and direction.
- You can sing the note names instead of the interval if you'd prefer. Instead of "one, five," you could use the exact pitches. It's a great way to learn the notes on your instrument as well.

VISUALIZATION

Using your mind's eye is also part of the experience of ear training. Most instruments have patterns that represent a sound—a shape you can memorize that is a certain interval. For instance, on an electric bass, intervals can be played using geometric patterns that repeat all over the fretboard. A piano has the distance of keys—a major 3rd is always four keys up when ascending and eight keys down when descending. You can visualize the patterns like the fingering shapes on a guitar or on a wind instrument. Guitars have movable patterns for chords and scales that can be memorized and visualized. As we learn to identify intervals, we visualize how they are mapped on our instrument. Visualize the shape with the sound in your mind's eye.

5. Visualization Exercise

To visualize, we want to associate a shape or pattern on our instrument with a sound. This will enable us to hear patterns and instinctively have them at our fingertips.

1. Grab your instrument and play the tonic.
2. Visualize/notice the interval's location on your instrument and sing the interval aloud.
3. Play the interval on your instrument.

Example: If practicing 5ths, play the tonic (on your instrument), visualize the location of the 5th on your instrument, sing the interval, and then play the 5th on your instrument to check the pitch you sang.

Options:

- Do this two ways: Tonic to interval and interval to tonic.
- Practice other shapes for the interval if they are available. For example, on bass guitar, an interval can have more than one shape on the fretboard. Associate these familiar shapes with the one interval sound.
- Chords and scales also have shapes. Memorize these shapes using visualization.

SENSATION/FEEL

When it comes to ear training, sensation and feeling can be a challenge to articulate. Emotions are very real, and we don't have a great measuring tool to define them. They are an interior quality, meaning they are part of our internal, subjective world; but there are identifying characteristics that manifest in the body. Researchers generally measure emotion by affective display or emotional expression. SCL (skin conductance level) measures the electrical conductivity of the skin. It reflects the level of physiological arousal elicited by cognition or emotions.

Sensation is a personal way of experiencing sound, an attempt to embody the sound in a feeling way. It is allowing the sensation of a tone, interval, or chord to interact with us and learning to recognize that interaction as a feeling or sense—whether it stirs emotion or makes the hair stand on the back of our necks. It's a "knowing" sensation that some players have a strong connection with or embody. It's knowing the right note or chord to play to create a feeling within or without—knowing an interval by the way it feels. This is the ability to sense and understand sound by being in touch with sensation and emotion.

6. Meditation Exercise

Each interval and chord introduced in this book will have a meditation track. Use these tracks any time you are open to slowing down your thoughts and experiencing the sounds at a deeper level.

1. Put away your phone or any other distraction so that you can focus clearly.
2. Sit or lie down and intend to be present in the moment.
3. Bring your attention to behind your eyes.
4. Start to breathe in a rhythmic way, counting your breaths: inhale for 5 seconds, hold your breath for 8 seconds, and exhale for 10 seconds. Play the Meditation Exercise.

 TRACK 13 Meditation Exercise

CREATIVE CONNECTION

Another way to enhance your ear training is to compose your own music using the interval, scale, or chord you are working on. This is a great way to practically apply what you are learning. Getting creative can lead to a greater familiarity and understanding of how notes sound melodically in a bass line, melody or part, and harmonically when played together as a chord.

7. Composition Exercise

Make time to sit with an interval and compose. It could be a bass part, a chord progression, or a melody. It's up to you—spend time exploring the sound and making music.

This is practice, not perfection. Play around and see what you can come up with. Make sure to sing along with the idea. You can use other notes, but focus on the interval you are working on.

Options:
- Create a bass line using the interval, intervals, chord tones, or scale.
- Create a melody using the interval, intervals, chord tones, or scale.
- Try a pedal tone, or drone note, using a repeated open string or fretted note over which you can play a riff or melody. You can also add a drone or pedal tone on another instrument and build an idea from that note.
- Create a riff or melody by playing two notes harmonically. Pay close attention to the tension and release that certain notes produce when played together.

CHAPTER 6:
Interval Practice

LET'S BEGIN

Let's start practicing intervals. **Get out your notebook and add your own notes for each interval as we go through them.** This is an important aspect of learning to discover things for yourself! We too easily gloss over material in a rush to get to the end result. Experiment and discover from your own experience. Don't assume that I've given you all you need—you have to be part of each experience. With ear training, there really are no shortcuts. It really is a process of learning to integrate how things sound. You have to do the work.

Each interval will include the following:

- **Characteristic:** Its sound or quality; the distance from the tonic and how it resonates.
- **Notes:** Ideas or observations that can be used to help remember things about the interval.
- **Reference:** A song or some example of the sound that you are familiar with so you can bring it forth in your mind's ear.

Included next for each interval is the Practice Template, the seven-step ear training method covered in the previous chapter. **It's not necessary for you to do each step every time.** For example, you may only need to do the Listening Exercise the first time you are working with a particular interval, or, you may not have time to sit down and do the Composition Exercise on a certain day.

Each interval will have a Listening Exercise, Mimic Exercise, Melodic Exercise, and Harmonic Exercise as a starting point. A meditation track will also be provided for the Meditation Exercise. The Visualization and Composition Exercises are for you to do on your own. Other suggestions and exercises will be added as we go. Ear training quizzes will be added throughout the book as well.

We'll begin with the perfect intervals. Download the Ascending Intervals PDF, listen to the audio, and fill out details in your notebook. I added character descriptions and notes that work for me. Sit with an interval until you can form your own ideas and make your own observations. As mentioned, each exercise will have its own audio track except for the Visualization and Composition exercises, which will be your responsibility to structure and complete.

 Ascending Intervals

UNISON AND OCTAVE

Characteristic: The unison is the same pitch, and the octave is twice the frequency. No conflict or rub.
Notes: Octaves are common in slap bass parts and Jazz guitar melodies.
Reference:
"Over the Rainbow" (*The Wizard of Oz*), **Some-where** over the rainbow
"Sweet Child O' Mine" (Guns N' Roses), first two notes of opening guitar riff
"Harry's Wondrous World" (*Harry Potter and the Sorcerer's Stone*), first two notes of opening melody
"Circle of Life" (*The Lion King*), In **the cir**-cle of life
"Rewrite the Stars" (*The Greatest Showman*), What if **we re**-write the starts? … Nothing **could keep** us apart

Practice Template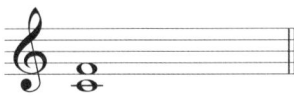

- ❏ TRACK 14 Listening Exercise
- ❏ TRACK 15 Mimic Exercise
- ❏ TRACK 16 Melodic Exercise
- ❏ TRACK 17 Harmonic Exercise
- ❏ Visualization Exercise
- ❏ TRACK 18 Meditation Exercise
- ❏ Composition Exercise

PERFECT 4TH

Characteristic: Open sounding. Stark. Pillar-like, but more gnomic than a 5th.
Notes: The first change in a blues progression.
Reference:
"Here Comes the Bride" (traditional wedding song), first two notes of melody
"Amazing Grace" (traditional hymn), **A-maz**-ing grace, how sweet the sound
"Eine Kleine Nachtmusik" (Mozart), opening notes of melody
"Jar of Hearts" (Christina Perri), And who do **you think** you are … you're gon-**na catch** a cold
"Do You Want to Build a Snowman?" (*Frozen*), Do you **want to build** a snowman? Come **on, let's go** and play

Practice Template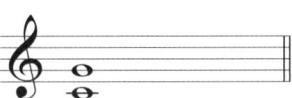

- ❏ TRACK 19 Listening Exercise
- ❏ TRACK 20 Mimic Exercise
- ❏ TRACK 21 Melodic Exercise
- ❏ TRACK 22 Harmonic Exercise
- ❏ Visualization Exercise
- ❏ TRACK 23 Meditation Exercise
- ❏ Composition Exercise

PERFECT 5TH

Characteristic: Open, clear sounding, wide, stable, and pillar-like. Grand. Majestic.
Notes: Bass parts are often built using a 1–5 pattern. When played as a double stop, the 5th is known as the "power chord" and is used in rock and heavy metal. Medieval or church-like in sound.
Reference:
"Star Wars (Main Theme)" (John Williams), opening notes
"Twinkle, Twinkle Little Star" (nursery rhyme), Twin-**kle twin**-kle little star
"Bad Romance" (Lady Gaga), Rah, **rah, ah**, ah, ah. Ro-**ma, ro**-ma, ma. Ga-**ga, ooh**-la la
"Speechless" (*Aladdin*, 2019), I won't be **si-lenced**. You can't keep me **qui-et**
"Easy on Me" (Adele), **Go eas**-y on me, babe

Practice Template

❏ TRACK 24 Listening Exercise	❏ Visualization Exercise
❏ TRACK 25 Mimic Exercise	❏ TRACK 28 Meditation Exercise
❏ TRACK 26 Melodic Exercise	❏ Composition Exercise
❏ TRACK 27 Harmonic Exercise	

🔊 **TRACK 29** Interval Quiz 1 (P1, P8, P4, P5)

MINOR 2ND

Characteristic: Harmonically, very dissonant and wobbly. Melodically, invasive and dark.
Notes: Called a semitone or half step.
Reference:
"Theme from Jaws" (John Williams), opening notes
"Isn't She Lovely" (Stevie Wonder), **Is-n't she** lovely
"A Hard Day's Night" (The Beatles), **It's been a** hard day's night
"A Sky Full of Stars" (Coldplay), **'Cause you're a** sky, **'cause you're a** sky full of stars
"What Was I Made For?" (Billie Eilish), What was I **made for**?

Practice Template

❏ TRACK 30 Listening Exercise	❏ Visualization Exercise
❏ TRACK 31 Mimic Exercise	❏ TRACK 34 Meditation Exercise
❏ TRACK 32 Melodic Exercise	❏ Composition Exercise
❏ TRACK 33 Harmonic Exercise	

MAJOR 2ND

Characteristic: Harmonically, slightly dissonant and close. Melodically, close and ambiguous but building.
Notes: Whole tone. A big clue for this sound is that it is the second note of a major scale.
Reference:
"Happy Birthday to You" (traditional birthday song), Hap-**py birth-day** to you
"Do-Re-Mi" (*The Sound of Music*), **Doe, a deer,** a female deer
"Shape of You" (Ed Sheeran), **I'm in** love with the **shape of** you. We **push and** pull like a **mag-net** do
"Whole New World" (*Aladdin*), A whole **new world**
"Silent Night" (Christmas song), **Si**-lent night, **ho**-ly night

Practice Template

- ❏ **TRACK 35** Listening Exercise
- ❏ **TRACK 36** Mimic Exercise
- ❏ **TRACK 37** Melodic Exercise
- ❏ **TRACK 38** Harmonic Exercise
- ❏ Visualization Exercise
- ❏ **TRACK 39** Meditation Exercise
- ❏ Composition Exercise

🔊 **TRACK 40** Interval Quiz 2 (P1, P8, m2, M2, P4, P5)

MINOR 3RD

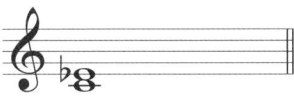

Characteristic: Harmonically, dark and mellow. Melodically, emotive and longing.
Notes: A very common sound. Easy to hear and has gravity.
Reference:
"Greensleeves" (English folk song), first two notes of melody
"Smoke on the Water" (Deep Purple), first two notes of opening guitar riff
"Whole Lotta Love" (Led Zeppelin), opening guitar riff
The Hunger Games whistle signal, first two notes
"Peaches" (*The Super Mario Bros. Movie*), **peaches, peaches, peaches, peaches, peaches ...** (minor 3rds continue but moved up a whole step)

Practice Template

- ❏ **TRACK 41** Listening Exercise
- ❏ **TRACK 42** Mimic Exercise
- ❏ **TRACK 43** Melodic Exercise
- ❏ **TRACK 44** Harmonic Exercise
- ❏ Visualization Exercise
- ❏ **TRACK 45** Meditation Exercise
- ❏ Composition Exercise

MAJOR 3RD

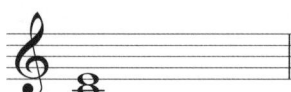

Characteristic: Harmonically, bright and solid. Melodically, calm and steady.
Notes: Chords are built from 3rds. Sound is as common as the 5th.
Reference:
"Kumbaya" (traditional spiritual), **Kum-ba**-ya, my Lord
"Spring" from *The Four Seasons* (Vivaldi), first two notes of melody
"Some Nights" (fun.), Some nights **I stay** up cash-in' in my bad luck
"Firework" (Katy Perry), 'Cause, baby, you're a fi-**re-work**. Come on, show 'em what **you're worth**
"Havana" (Camila Cabello), **Ha-van**-a ohh na na

Practice Template

- ❏ **TRACK 46** Listening Exercise
- ❏ **TRACK 47** Mimic Exercise
- ❏ **TRACK 48** Melodic Exercise
- ❏ **TRACK 49** Harmonic Exercise
- ❏ Visualization Exercise
- ❏ **TRACK 50** Meditation Exercise
- ❏ Composition Exercise

 TRACK 51 Interval Quiz 3 (P1, P8, m2, M2, m3, M3, P4, P5)

MINOR 6TH

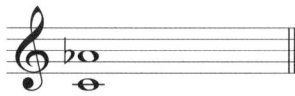

Characteristic: Harmonically and melodically mysterious and inquisitive.
Notes: Same as an augmented 5th.
Reference:
"Black Orpheus (Manhã de Carnaval)" (Luiz Bonfá), first two notes of melody
"The Entertainer" (Joplin), second and third alternating notes
"Golden Hour" (JVKE), It's **your gold**-en hour
"No Time to Die" (Billie Eilish), **That I'd** fallen for a lie? **You were** never on my side

Practice Template

- ❏ **TRACK 52** Listening Exercise
- ❏ **TRACK 53** Mimic Exercise
- ❏ **TRACK 54** Melodic Exercise
- ❏ **TRACK 55** Harmonic Exercise
- ❏ Visualization Exercise
- ❏ **TRACK 56** Meditation Exercise
- ❏ Composition Exercise

MAJOR 6TH

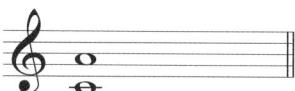

Characteristic: Harmonically, stable and dramatic. Melodically, inquisitive and rich.
Notes: Common note used as beat 4 of a major walking bass part.
Reference:
"Hush Little Baby" (nursery rhyme), **Hush little** baby don't say a word
"Jingle Bells" (Christmas song), **Dash-ing** through the snow
"Sweet Caroline" (Neil Diamond), **Sweet Car**-o-line
"Glimpse of Us" (Joji), 'Cause sometimes I look in her eyes, and that's where I find **a glimpse** of us

Practice Template

- ❏ **TRACK 57** Listening Exercise
- ❏ **TRACK 58** Mimic Exercise
- ❏ **TRACK 59** Melodic Exercise
- ❏ **TRACK 60** Harmonic Exercise
- ❏ Visualization Exercise
- ❏ **TRACK 61** Meditation Exercise
- ❏ Composition Exercise

 TRACK 62 Interval Quiz 4 (P1, P8, m2, M2, m3, M3, P4, P5, m6, M6)

MINOR 7TH

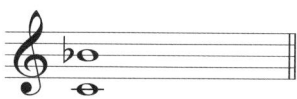

Characteristic: Harmonically, questioning. Wide gap. Melodically, static and funky sounding.
Notes: Used in a lot of funky bass parts.
Reference:
"Josie" (Steely Dan), first two notes of opening guitar riff
"The Winner Takes It All" (ABBA), The **win-ner** takes it all
"Chameleon" (Herbie Hancock), bass pattern jumps from the root to a minor 7th then to an octave
"Somewhere" (*West Side Story*), **There's a** place for us

Practice Template

- ❏ **TRACK 63** Listening Exercise
- ❏ **TRACK 64** Mimic Exercise
- ❏ **TRACK 65** Melodic Exercise
- ❏ **TRACK 66** Harmonic Exercise
- ❏ Visualization Exercise
- ❏ **TRACK 67** Meditation Exercise
- ❏ Composition Exercise

MAJOR 7TH

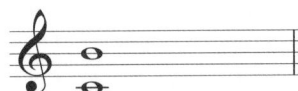

Characteristic: Harmonically, dissonant and distant. Melodically, wide and piercing, pushes to resolve upward.
Notes: "Ti" to "Do" is apparent.
Reference:
"Don't Know Why" (Norah Jones), **I wait**-ed till I saw the sun
"Take on Me" (A-ha), **Take on** me (Take on me)
"Perfect" (Hedley), I'm **not per**-fect, but I **keep try**-ing

Practice Template

- ❏ TRACK 68 Listening Exercise
- ❏ TRACK 69 Mimic Exercise
- ❏ TRACK 70 Melodic Exercise
- ❏ TRACK 71 Harmonic Exercise
- ❏ Visualization Exercise
- ❏ TRACK 72 Meditation Exercise
- ❏ Composition Exercise

 TRACK 73 Interval Quiz 5 (P1, P8, m2, M2, m3, M3, P4, P5, m6, M6, m7, M7)

DIMINISHED 5TH/AUGMENTED 4TH

Characteristic: Mysterious and dark, but bright. Melodically bluesy.
Notes: The tritone ("tri" = 3 whole steps). Same distance as an augmented 4th. Dark when used with a minor 3rd; sci-fi when used with a major 3rd.
Reference:
"Theme from *The Simpsons*" (Danny Elfman), **The simp**-sons
"Isotope" (Joe Henderson), pickup note into the first note of the melody
"Symptom of the Universe" (Black Sabbath), opening guitar riff
"The Carney" (Nick Cave), main piano riff

Practice Template

- ❏ TRACK 74 Listening Exercise
- ❏ TRACK 75 Mimic Exercise
- ❏ TRACK 76 Melodic Exercise
- ❏ TRACK 77 Harmonic Exercise
- ❏ Visualization Exercise
- ❏ TRACK 78 Meditation Exercise
- ❏ Composition Exercise

AUGMENTED 5TH

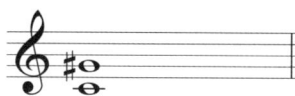

Characteristic: Mysterious sounding.
Notes: Same as a minor 6th.
Reference:
"Black Orpheus (Manhã de Carnaval)" (Luiz Bonfá), first two notes of melody
"The Entertainer" (Joplin), second and third alternating notes
"Golden Hour" (JVKE), It's **your gold**-en hour
"No Time to Die" (Billie Eilish), **That I'd** fallen for a lie? **You were** never on my side

Practice Template

- ❏ TRACK 79 Listening Exercise
- ❏ TRACK 80 Mimic Exercise
- ❏ TRACK 81 Melodic Exercise
- ❏ TRACK 82 Harmonic Exercise
- ❏ Visualization Exercise
- ❏ TRACK 83 Meditation Exercise
- ❏ Composition Exercise

 TRACK 84 Interval Quiz 6 (P1, P8, m2, M2, m3, M3, P4, P5, d5, m6 or A5, M6, m7, M7)

CHAPTER 7:
Scale Practice

Learning how to hear the sound of a scale is great for melodic reasons and our continued work on interval recognition. In this chapter, we will work on how intervals relate within a particular scale. Continue to use the Practice Template but without the Harmonic Exercise (because a scale is a melodic treatment of intervals). In do-it-yourself fashion, add or remove elements as needed.

SCALE TYPES

Remember, a musical scale is an organized set of notes or pitches that span an octave. There are many types of scales, but the *major scale* is the template from which all other scales can be understood and defined. The scale degrees of a major scale are 1-2-3-4-5-6-7-8. Other scales are defined by modifying those scale degrees with sharp (♯) or flat (♭) signs. (Remember, a sharp raises a note by a half step, and a flat lowers a note by a half step.) For example, a *minor scale* is 1-2-♭3-4-5-♭6-♭7-8.

Below is a list of scales you can use in your musical journey. (It's also in PDF form for download.) The list isn't something you need to have down before you proceed in this book. Explore how certain scales sound and use them to develop your musical ear and create your own music.

 Scale Types

SCALE TYPES	
Aeolian/Natural Minor	1 2 ♭3 4 5 ♭6 ♭7
Altered (Super Locrian)	1 ♭2 ♭3 ♭4 ♭5 ♭6 ♭7
Altered Japanese	1 2 3 4 5 ♭6
Arabic	1 2 3 4 ♭5 ♭6 ♭7
Augmented	1 ♯2 3 5 ♯5 7
Be Bop Dominant	1 2 3 4 5 6 ♭7 7
Blues	1 ♭3 4 ♭5 5 ♭7
Byzantine	1 ♭2 3 4 5 ♭6 7
Diminished	1 2 ♭3 4 5 ♭6 6 7
Dorian	1 2 ♭3 4 5 6 ♭7
Gypsy	1 2 ♭3 ♯4 5 ♭6 ♭7
Half-Diminished	1 2 ♭3 4 ♭5 ♭6 ♭7
Harmonic Major	1 2 3 4 5 ♭6 7
Hawaiian	1 2 ♭3 4 5 6 7
Hindu	1 2 3 4 5 ♭6 ♭7
Hungarian Major	1 ♯2 3 ♯4 5 6 ♭7
Hungarian Minor	1 2 ♭3 ♯4 5 ♭6 7
Japanese	1 ♭2 4 5 ♭6
Javanese	1 ♭2 ♭3 4 5 6 ♭7

SCALE TYPES	
Jazz Melodic Minor	1 2 ♭3 4 5 6 7
Major (Ionian)	1 2 3 4 5 6 7
Locrian	1 ♭2 ♭3 4 ♭5 ♭6 ♭7
Locrian Major	1 2 3 4 ♭5 ♭6 ♭7
Lydian	1 2 3 ♯4 5 6 7
Lydian Augmented	1 2 3 ♯4 ♯5 6 7
Lydian Dominant/Acoustic	1 2 3 ♯4 5 6 ♭7
Melodic Minor	A: 1 2 ♭3 4 5 6 7 D: ♭7 ♭6 5 4 ♭3 2 1
Mixolydian	1 2 3 4 5 6 ♭7
Neapolitan Major	1 ♭2 ♭3 4 5 6 7
Persian	1 ♭2 3 4 ♭5 ♭6 7
Phrygian	1 ♭2 ♭3 4 5 ♭6 ♭7
Phrygian Dominant	1 ♭2 3 4 5 ♭6 ♭7
Spanish	1 ♭2 3 4 ♭5 ♭6 7
Symmetrical Diminished/Octatonic	1 ♭2 ♭3 3 ♯4 5 6 ♭7
Whole Tone	1 2 3 ♯4 ♯5 ♯6

We will use the major and minor scales as examples of how to practice ear training for scales. Scale recognition is the best way to describe what we'll be doing. Learning to recognize the sound of a particular scale helps when you are working with melodies and other linear material. In the previous chapter, we worked on intervals in relation to a tonic or key center. The audio from the practice template will step you through the process.

MAJOR SCALE

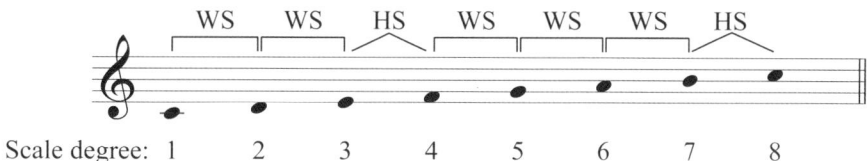

Characteristic: Bright and pleasant sounding when played in a sequence.
Notes: All scales can be defined using the major scale. Modal harmony is built from the major scale.
Reference: "I Want You Back" (The Jackson 5) with a few added chromatic notes, "Ode to Joy" (Beethoven), "Lean on Me" (Bill Withers), "Happy Birthday to You" (traditional birthday song), "Lift Me Up" (*Black Panther: Wakanda Forever*), "How Far I'll Go" (*Moana*)

Practice Template

- ❏ TRACK 85 Listening Exercise
- ❏ TRACK 86 Mimic Exercise 1
- ❏ TRACK 87 Mimic Exercise 2
- ❏ TRACK 88 Melodic Exercise
- ❏ Visualization Exercise
- ❏ TRACK 89 Meditation Exercise
- ❏ Composition Exercise

BROKEN INTERVALS

A common practice when working with scales is to break them up into interval practice. After each note of the scale—as you ascend or descend—insert the chosen interval note from the scale. Breaking up the intervals in this way shows the relationships among other notes in the scale. (Note: The following examples go higher than the octave of the tonic for a sense of completion to each pattern.)

3rds
Starting with 3rds is a great way to see how the major scale is full of major and minor 3rd relationships.

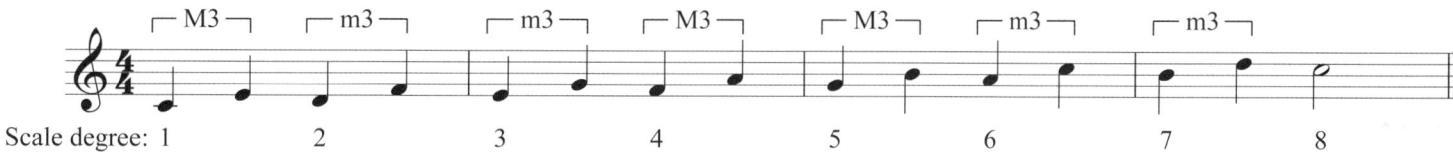

Practice Template

- ❏ TRACK 90 Listening Exercise
- ❏ TRACK 91 Mimic Exercise
- ❏ TRACK 92 Melodic Exercise
- ❏ Visualization Exercise

4ths

Notice the one augmented 4th within the scale.

Scale degree: 1 2 3 4 5 6 7 8

Practice Template

- TRACK 93 Listening Exercise
- TRACK 94 Mimic Exercise
- TRACK 95 Melodic Exercise
- Visualization Exercise

5ths

In a major scale, all 5ths are perfect except for one diminished 5th.

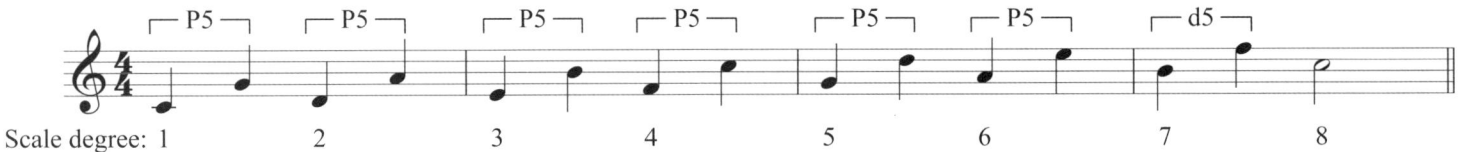

Scale degree: 1 2 3 4 5 6 7 8

Practice Template

- TRACK 96 Listening Exercise
- TRACK 97 Mimic Exercise
- TRACK 98 Melodic Exercise
- Visualization Exercise

6ths

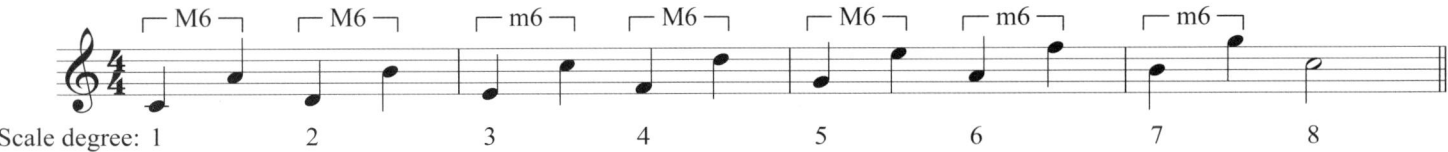

Scale degree: 1 2 3 4 5 6 7 8

Practice Template

- TRACK 99 Listening Exercise
- TRACK 100 Mimic Exercise
- TRACK 101 Melodic Exercise
- Visualization Exercise

46

7ths

Scale degree: 1 2 3 4 5 6 7 8

Practice Template

- ❏ TRACK 102 Listening Exercise
- ❏ TRACK 103 Mimic Exercise
- ❏ TRACK 104 Melodic Exercise
- ❏ Visualization Exercise

MINOR SCALE

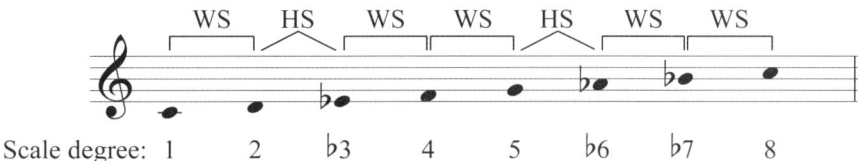

Scale degree: 1 2 ♭3 4 5 ♭6 ♭7 8

Characteristic: Dark and subdued sound. The flat 6 creates a moodier vibe, almost unusual or mystical.
Notes: Relative minor key, 6th degree of the major scale.
Reference: "My Favorite Things" (*The Sound of Music*), "Sweet Dreams" (The Eurythmics), "I Shot the Sheriff" (Bob Marley), "Crazy Train" (Ozzy Osbourne), "We Don't Talk About Bruno" (*Encanto*), "Happier Than Ever" (Billie Eilish)

Practice Template

- ❏ TRACK 105 Listening Exercise
- ❏ TRACK 106 Mimic Exercise 1
- ❏ TRACK 107 Mimic Exercise 2
- ❏ TRACK 108 Melodic Exercise
- ❏ Visualization Exercise
- ❏ TRACK 109 Meditation Exercise
- ❏ Composition Exercise

DESIRABLE DIFFICULTY—BROKEN INTERVALS

You've most likely heard the phrase "no pain, no gain" in regard to physical growth when exercising. Maybe it's not the most concise phrase to explain muscle burn, but it encapsulates the idea that one must work reasonably hard for the best results. The phrase applies to mental exercise too. When learning is more challenging, it requires you to focus more on each idea, causing your brain to strengthen connections between neural pathways for later recall. Brain scientists have a term called "desirable difficulty" to describe the fact that peak learning and retention go hand in hand with a little bit of difficulty. When the going gets tough, push through—you are learning! The personal "rub" is for you to stay engaged with the difficulty or challenge when learning new things.

Assignment: Minor Scale Broken Intervals (3rds, 4ths, 5ths, 6ths, and 7ths)

Now take the minor scale and practice it in broken intervals. Write it down and take the time to understand and hear what you are doing. Notice whether any internal resistance arises and push through. Make this a welcome challenge for yourself. Write out all the broken intervals (3rds-7ths) before you check the PDF handout.

 Minor Scale Broken Intervals Answers

FOLLOW THE ROOT

Following the bass movement in a song is a great way to practice ear training. The bass generally outlines the chord progression and gives the basic tonal structure of a song. The *root note* is the note that a chord is built on and from which it gets its name. (For example, the root note of a C chord is the note C.) You can play along with the root notes of chords on any instrument. This can be a great exercise to warm up with. If you are a gigging musician, you can do this to get to know songs from the bottom up. It's a great way to learn and memorize tunes while practicing intervals. (Note: We'll get more into chord theory in Chapters 9 and 10.)

CHAPTER 8:
Descending Interval Practice

To get the most out of this learning experience, make sure you are very familiar with the ascending interval sounds before working on the descending interval sounds in this chapter.

DESCENDING RELATIONSHIPS

Intervals, chords, and scales are built from the tonic or root upward. This bottom-up approach can make hearing descending intervals a little tricky. Each descending interval (meaning downward from the octave of the tonic) has an equivalent ascending relationship. For example, a descending minor 3rd is the same note as an ascending major 6th. In the key of C, the major 6th is an A, but the octave of C down to A is a minor 3rd. The ascending/descending interval pairs are shown below.

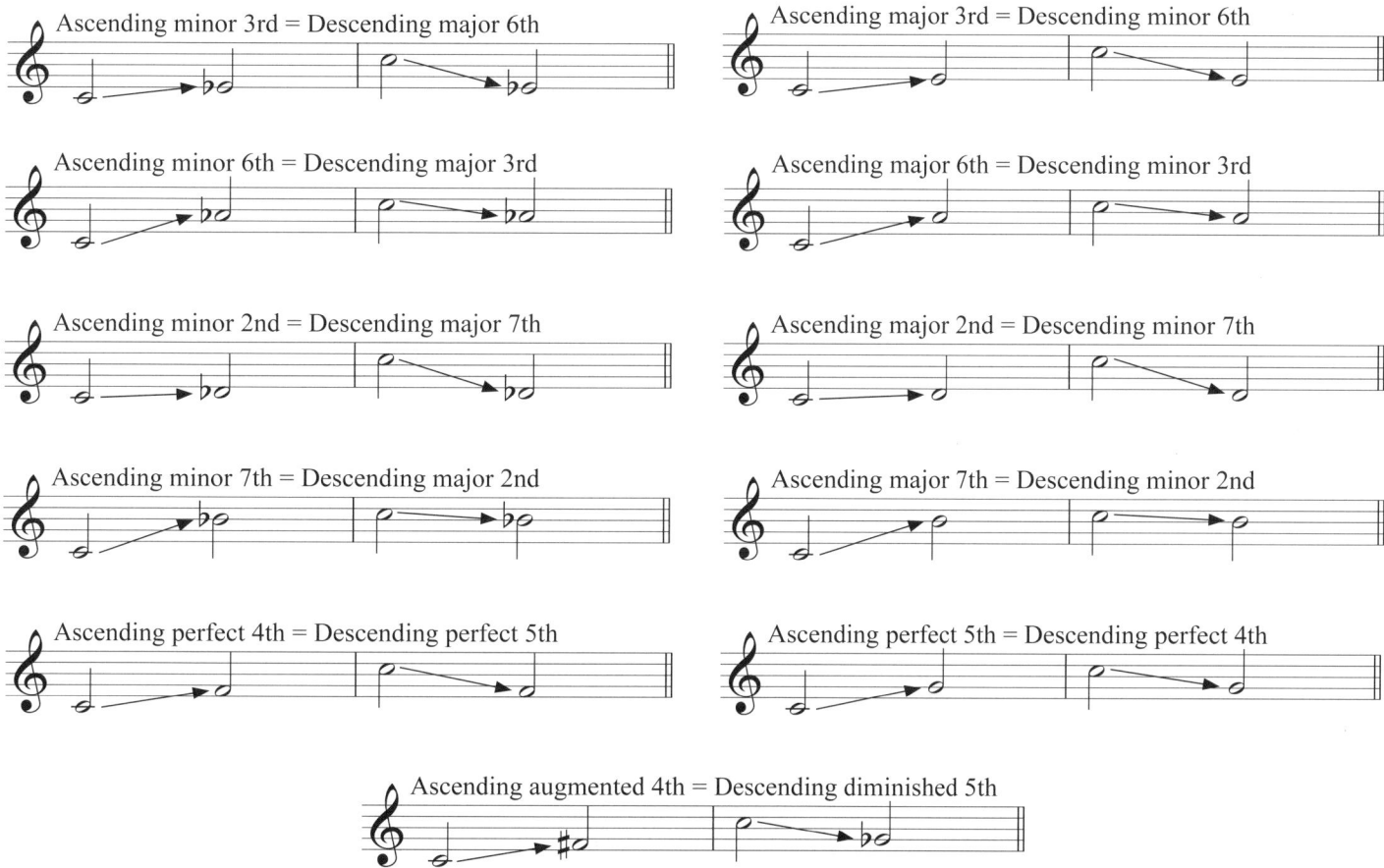

If an ascending interval is minor, its descending interval will be major; if it ascends as a major interval, it will descend as a minor interval. All you really need to do is memorize this: 2nds go with 7ths and 3rds go with 6ths, in either direction. The tritone is symmetric and is the same sound in either direction.

THE MATH

We all love math, don't we? The mathematical key for these relationships is the number 9; both intervals added together equal 9. Also, the quality is opposite—major to minor, minor to major, etc. For example, if you want to find the descending equivalent for a minor 2nd, subtract 2 from 9, change the quality to major, and you get a major 7th. The same is true for diminished and augmented intervals, but no math is necessary for the tritone. Because the tritone is right in the middle of the scale, it is the same distance ascending and descending.

UP AND DOWN PRACTICE

You've done the work (hopefully) to master ascending intervals. Now it's time to solidify and memorize the descending correlation to the ascending interval.

A great practice to cement the ascending/descending interval-pair relationship is to practice them together: tonic, interval up, tonic, interval down, tonic. This is a mimic exercise. In true do-it-yourself fashion, it's time to branch off on your own. After each mimic exercise, the tonic will be played for you to hum or sing the sequence. Continue by yourself with a melodic audiation. Play the tonic and practice singing the sequence you just practiced or play the octave and sing down to the tonic. Sing or hum an octave lower if needed. You can practice this exercise with your instrument, using your instrument to check pitches after you sing.

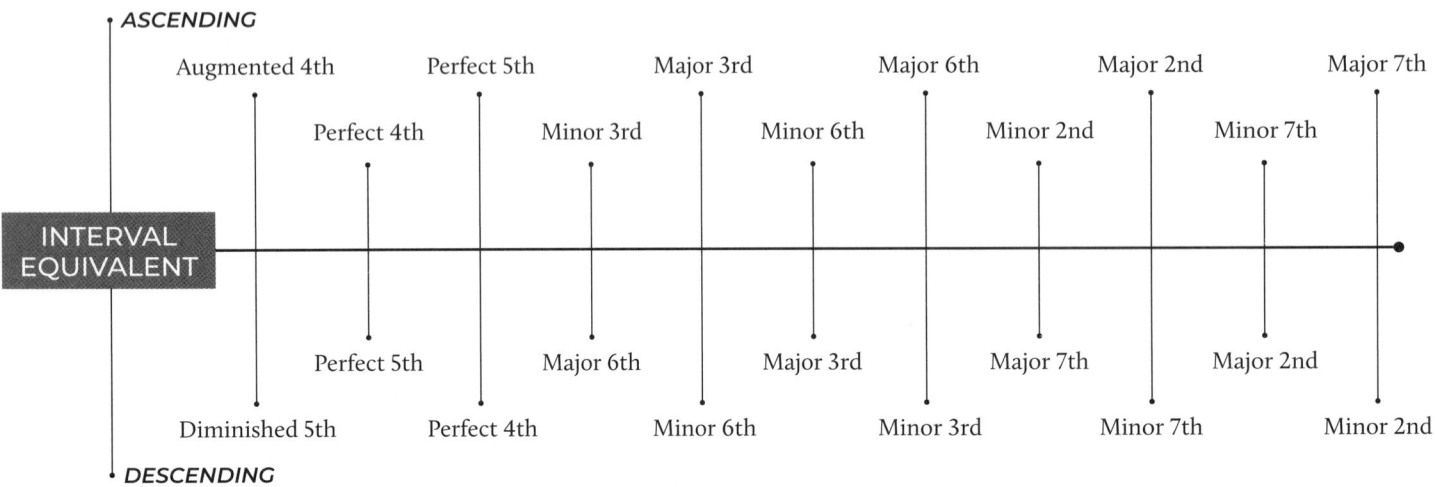

- **TRACK 110** Ascending Augmented 4th/Descending Diminished 5th
- **TRACK 111** Ascending Perfect 4th/ Descending Perfect 5th
- **TRACK 112** Ascending Perfect 5th/Descending Perfect 4th
- **TRACK 113** Ascending Minor 3rd/Descending Major 6th
- **TRACK 114** Ascending Major 3rd/Descending Minor 6th
- **TRACK 115** Ascending Minor 6th/Descending Major 3rd
- **TRACK 116** Ascending Major 6th/Descending Minor 3rd
- **TRACK 117** Ascending Minor 2nd/Descending Major 7th
- **TRACK 118** Ascending Major 2nd/Descending Minor 7th
- **TRACK 119** Ascending Minor 7th/Descending Major 2nd
- **TRACK 120** Ascending Major 7th/Descending Minor 2nd

DESCENDING PRACTICE

You've had the ascending intervals as a guide. Download the Descending Intervals PDF to fill out characteristics, notes, and references. References are plentiful if you look online for inspiration and ideas.

Descending Intervals

TRACK 121 Descending Interval Quiz 1 (P1, P8, P4, P5)

TRACK 122 Descending Interval Quiz 2 (P1, P8, m2, M2, P4, P5)

TRACK 123 Descending Interval Quiz 3 (P1, P8, m2, M2, m3, M3, P4, P5)

TRACK 124 Descending Interval Quiz 4 (P1, P8, m2, M2, m3, M3, P4, P5, m6, M6)

TRACK 125 Descending Interval Quiz 5 (P1, P8, m2, M2, m3, M3, P4, P5, m6, M6, m7, M7)

ASCENDING AND DESCENDING INTERVALS

Let's do some drills focusing on intervals in both directions.

TRACK 126 Up and Down Interval Quiz 1 (P1, P8, P4, P5)

TRACK 127 Up and Down Interval Quiz 2 (P1, P8, m2, M2, P4, P5)

TRACK 128 Up and Down Interval Quiz 3 (P1, P8, m2, M2, m3, M3, P4, P5)

TRACK 129 Up and Down Interval Quiz 4 (P1, P8, m2, M2, m3, M3, P4, P5, m6, M6)

TRACK 130 Up and Down Interval Quiz 5 (P1, P8, m2, M2, m3, M3, P4, P5, m6, M6, m7, M7)

CHAPTER 9:
Triad Theory and Practice

A *triad* is a three-note chord made up of the root, 3rd, and 5th. A triad is a "stack" of 3rds—from the root to the 3rd is the distance of a 3rd, and from the 3rd to the 5th is the distance of a 3rd. The quality of each 3rd in the stack is either major or minor depending on the type of triad.

FOUR TYPES OF TRIADS

Major Triad (1–3–5)

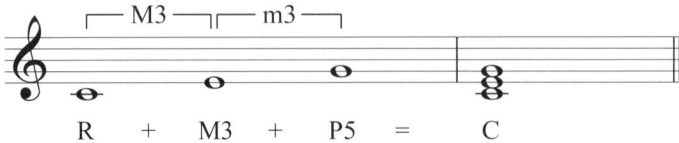

Minor Triad (1–♭3–5)

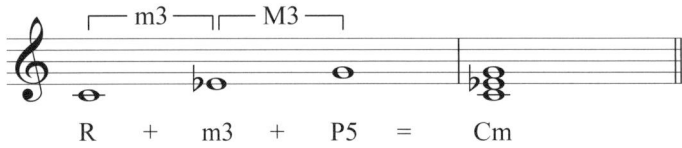

Diminished Triad (1–♭3–♭5)

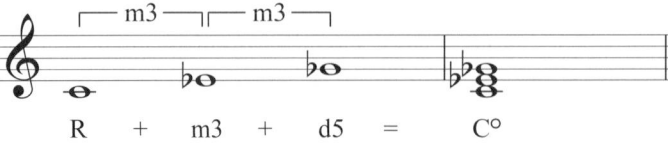

Augmented Triad (1–3–♯5)

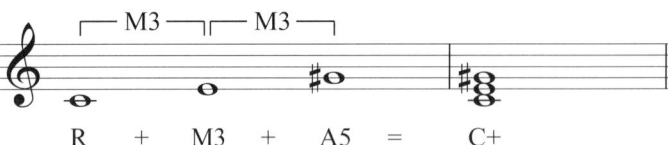

LABELING TRIADS (CHORD SYMBOLS)

To show the different *chord symbols*, or ways to label triads in written music, we'll use C as the example root note. A major triad is indicated with *just* the root note (C, for instance).

Major	C, Cmaj, C△
Minor	Cm, C-
Diminished	C°, Cdim
Augmented	C+, Caug

Practicing triads is very much the same as practicing intervals except we are adding a third note to the mix. Follow the seven-step ear training template. Get your notebook out, *listen*, and take notes. Discover for yourself!

 Triads

FILLING IN THE INFORMATION/DOING THE WORK

So far, I have completed all the information regarding characteristics, notes, and references for each interval. It is crucial to rely on your own experiences and opinions rather than simply adopting others' perceptions. Now it's your turn to fill in these fields for the remaining intervals and chords in the book. Take some time and do the research; you'll only strengthen your ears and awareness by looking for references for each new topic. If you haven't provided your own interpretations for the earlier examples, I strongly urge you to do so.

MAJOR TRIAD

Characteristic: _____

_____

Notes: _____

_____

Reference: _____

_____

Practice Template 🔊

- ❏ **TRACK 131** Listening Exercise
- ❏ **TRACK 132** Mimic Exercise
- ❏ **TRACK 133** Melodic Exercise
- ❏ **TRACK 134** Harmonic Exercise
- ❏ Visualization Exercise
- ❏ **TRACK 135** Meditation Exercise
- ❏ Composition Exercise

MINOR TRIAD

Characteristic: _____

_____

Notes: _____

_____

Reference: _____

_____

Practice Template 🔊

- ❏ **TRACK 136** Listening Exercise
- ❏ **TRACK 137** Mimic Exercise
- ❏ **TRACK 138** Melodic Exercise
- ❏ **TRACK 139** Harmonic Exercise
- ❏ Visualization Exercise
- ❏ **TRACK 140** Meditation Exercise
- ❏ Composition Exercise

🔊 **TRACK 141** Triad Quiz 1 (major or minor)

DIMINISHED TRIAD

Characteristic: _____

_____

Notes: _____

_____

Reference: _____

_____

Practice Template 🔊

- ❏ **TRACK 142** Listening Exercise
- ❏ **TRACK 143** Mimic Exercise
- ❏ **TRACK 144** Melodic Exercise
- ❏ **TRACK 145** Harmonic Exercise
- ❏ Visualization Exercise
- ❏ **TRACK 146** Meditation Exercise
- ❏ Composition Exercise

AUGMENTED TRIAD

Characteristic: _____

Notes: _____

Reference: _____

Practice Template 🔊

- ❏ **TRACK 147** Listening Exercise
- ❏ **TRACK 148** Mimic Exercise
- ❏ **TRACK 149** Melodic Exercise
- ❏ **TRACK 150** Harmonic Exercise
- ❏ Visualization Exercise
- ❏ **TRACK 151** Meditation Exercise
- ❏ Composition Exercise

🔊 **TRACK 152 Triad Quiz 2** (diminished or augmented)

🔊 **TRACK 153 Triad Quiz 3** (major, minor, diminished, or augmented)

OTHER TRIAD PRACTICE

Middle Note

Remember, triads are stacks of 3rds. They offer a great opportunity to practice singing 3rds starting at the 3rd of a triad.

1. Grab your instrument, play the 3rd, and sing it.
2. Sing up to the 5th.
3. Sing the 3rd.
4. Sing down to the root.
5. Check with your instrument to see whether your pitches were correct.

Here is an example of this exercise using a major triad.

 TRACK 154 Major Triad Middle Note

Now you know what to do. Try the other triads yourself:

- Major Triad Middle Note
- Minor Triad Middle Note
- Diminished Triad Middle Note
- Augmented Triad Middle Note

Note: This is a great practice for major and minor 3rds ascending and descending! An augmented triad is a major 3rd up and down if you start at the 3rd. A diminished triad is a minor 3rd up and down if you start at the 3rd. This is probably the best practice for 3rds because you are covering ascending and descending in the same exercise while hearing augmented and diminished tonalities.

Harmonic Triad Drill

Hearing the notes in a chord and picking them out is extremely helpful and a good practice.

1. Grab an instrument that can play more than one note at a time and play the triad harmonically.
2. Hold the chord.
3. Sing the notes in the triad.
4. Check yourself melodically on your instrument.

Here is an example of a major triad using this harmonic technique.

 TRACK 155 Major Triad Harmonic Drill (Root–3rd–5th)

Variations

There are six different variations you can practice. If you want to surprise yourself, get a six-sided die and practice singing the one that comes up when you roll.

- root–3rd–5th
- root–5th–3rd
- 3rd–root–5th
- 3rd–5th–root
- 5th–3rd–root
- 5th–root–3rd

Now that you are familiar with how to do this ... roll the die.

- Major Triad Harmonic Drill
- Minor Triad Harmonic Drill
- Diminished Triad Harmonic Drill
- Augmented Triad Harmonic Drill

MOVING FORWARD

It's time for the training wheels to come off; now, it's on you to keep things rolling. Review the previous chapters if you feel stuck in any way—musically, motivationally, or otherwise—and use your creativity to expand on ideas from this book.

> *"If you are not willing to learn, no one can help you.*
> *If you are determined to learn, no one can stop you."*
> —Zig Ziglar

SUSPENDED CHORDS

Another three-note chord to practice is a *suspended*, or *sus*, chord. A sus chord replaces the 3rd interval with either a 4th (sus4) or 2nd (sus2). Now, apply the practice methods discussed earlier to these two chords.

Sus4 Chord (1–4–5)

The interval distances for a sus4 chord is a perfect 4th from the root to the 4th and a major 2nd from the 4th to the 5th. The lack of a third in a suspended chord creates an open sound and the dissonance from the major second creates tension.

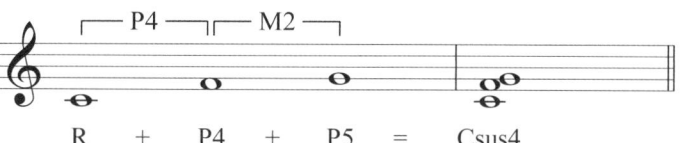

Characteristic: _____

_____

Notes: _____

_____

Reference: _____

_____

 **TRACK 156** Sus4 Listening Exercise

Sus2 Chord (1–2–5)

The sus2 chord starts with a major second interval from the root to the 2nd and a perfect 4th from the 2nd to the 5th.

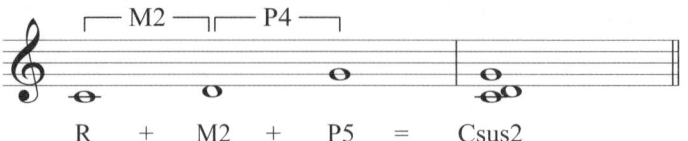

Characteristic: _____

_____

Notes: _____

_____

Reference: _____

_____

 TRACK 157 Sus2 Listening Exercise

 TRACK 158 Sus Quiz 1 (sus4, sus2)

TRIAD INVERSIONS

A triad with the root note as the lowest note and stacked 1–3–5 is in *root position*. If we stack a chord with another interval as the lowest note, we call that an *inversion*. If the 3rd is the lowest note, it is in *first inversion*; if the 5th is on the bottom, it is in *second inversion*. When chords are stacked using different inversions, the interval distance shifts. For example, in a first-inversion major triad, the 5th to the octave (root) is a perfect 4th in distance. A great way to practice different inversions is to sing them descending from the highest note to the lowest. Practice hearing the different inversions harmonically and melodically.

 TRACK 159 Triad Inversion Listening Exercise

Root Position (1-3-5)   First Inversion (3-5-1)   Second Inversion (5-1-3)

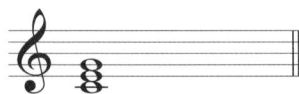 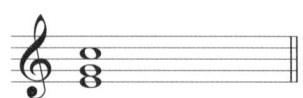 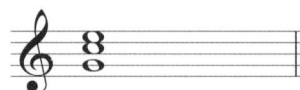

CHAPTER 10:
Seventh Chords

A *seventh chord* (*7th chord* or *7 chord*) is a chord with guess what on top? A 7th? That's right! The added 7th interval on top continues the stacking of 3rds pattern we learned about with triads. Remember? A triad is a stack of 3rds—root to 3rd, 3rd to 5th; now, with seventh chords, we add 5th to 7th. Here are the four most common seventh chords used in music:

Major 7 (1–3–5–7)

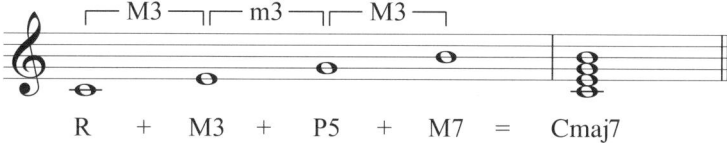

Minor 7 (1–♭3–5–♭7)

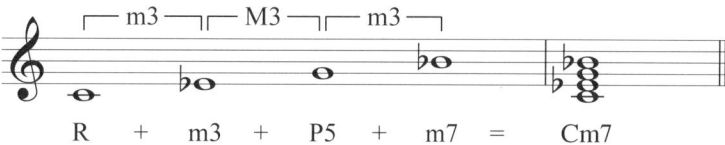

Dominant 7 (1–3–5–♭7)

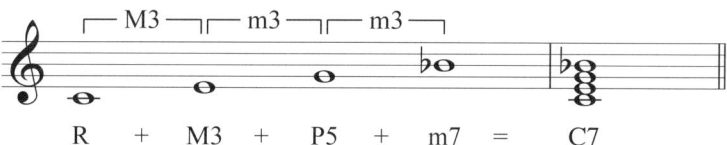

Minor 7♭5 (1–♭3–♭5–♭7)

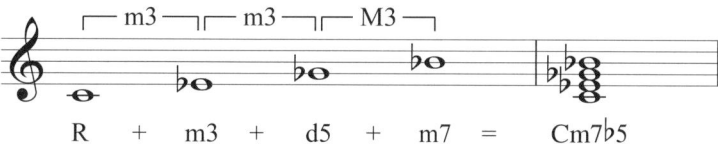

LABELING SEVENTH CHORDS

There are various chord symbols used to identify seventh chords. We'll use C as the example root note.

Major 7	Cmaj7, CΔ7
Minor 7	Cm7, C-7
Dominant 7	C7
Minor 7♭5	Cm7♭5, C⌀7

Now, follow the seven-step ear training template for seventh chords. Remember, you are the one filling in all of the information. Take your time and be curious when listening.

Seventh Chords

MAJOR 7

Characteristic: _____

_____

Notes: _____

_____

Reference: _____

_____

Practice Template 🔊

- ❏ TRACK 160 Listening Exercise
- ❏ TRACK 161 Mimic Exercise
- ❏ TRACK 162 Melodic Exercise
- ❏ TRACK 163 Harmonic Exercise
- ❏ Visualization Exercise
- ❏ TRACK 164 Meditation Exercise
- ❏ Composition Exercise

MINOR 7

Characteristic: _____

_____

Notes: _____

_____

Reference: _____

_____

Practice Template 🔊

- ❏ **TRACK 165** Listening Exercise
- ❏ **TRACK 166** Mimic Exercise
- ❏ **TRACK 167** Melodic Exercise
- ❏ **TRACK 168** Harmonic Exercise
- ❏ Visualization Exercise
- ❏ **TRACK 169** Meditation Exercise
- ❏ Composition Exercise

🔊 **TRACK 170** Seventh Chord Quiz 1 (major 7 or minor 7)

DOMINANT 7

Characteristic: _____

_____

Notes: _____

Reference: _____

_____

Practice Template 🔊

- ❏ **TRACK 171** Listening Exercise
- ❏ **TRACK 172** Mimic Exercise
- ❏ **TRACK 173** Melodic Exercise
- ❏ **TRACK 174** Harmonic Exercise
- ❏ Visualization Exercise
- ❏ **TRACK 175** Meditation Exercise
- ❏ Composition Exercise

🔊 **TRACK 176** Seventh Chord Quiz 2 (major 7, minor 7, or dominant 7)

MINOR 7♭5

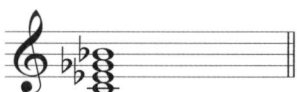

Characteristic: _____

_____

Notes: _____

_____

Reference: _____

_____

Practice Template 🔊

- ❏ TRACK 177 Listening Exercise
- ❏ TRACK 178 Mimic Exercise
- ❏ TRACK 179 Melodic Exercise
- ❏ TRACK 180 Harmonic Exercise
- ❏ Visualization Exercise
- ❏ TRACK 181 Meditation Exercise
- ❏ Composition Exercise

🔊 **TRACK 182** Seventh Chord Quiz 3 (major 7, minor 7, dominant 7, or minor 7♭5)

OTHER CHORD PRACTICE

Let's take the exercises we used with triads and extend them to seventh chords. Using creativity and problem-solving, you can create or modify existing exercises to meet any need.

> *"Creativity can solve almost any problem."—George Lois*

Melodic Middle Notes

This is a great exercise for any four-note chord. Start with either middle note—the 3rd or 5th—and sing up to the 7th and back down to the root.

1. Grab your instrument and play the 3rd or 5th and sing it.
2. Sing up to the 7th and then down to the root: 3–5–7–5–3–1 or 5–7–5–3–1.
3. Check the pitches against your instrument.

Here is an example of this exercise using a major seventh chord.

 TRACK 183 Middle Note Melodic Exercise (Major 7: 5–7–5–3–1)

Harmonic Middle Notes

Hearing the notes in a chord and picking them out is extremely helpful and a good practice. We've been doing this with each Harmonic Exercise. In this variation, keep the chord held and sing the notes in the chord.

1. Grab an instrument that's capable of chord playing and play a seventh chord.
2. Hold the chord.
3. Sing the notes in the chord.
4. Check yourself melodically on your instrument.

Here is an example of this harmonic technique using a major seventh chord.

 TRACK 184 Middle Note Harmonic Exercise (Major 7: 3-5-7-5-3-1)

In the triad section, we looked at different variations you can sing when doing this exercise. Mix this exercise up with different starting notes. Write out the variations you can practice, adding the 7th.

SUSPENDED 7 CHORDS

Adding a minor seventh to a sus2 or sus4 chord is commonplace in the music world. It's almost always a minor seventh degree in a sus chord. The chords are neither major or minor because they lack a third and are written as seventh chords like a dominant chord due to the flatted seventh degree.

 Sus Chords

7sus4

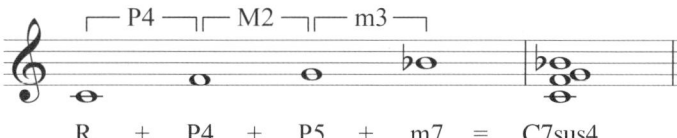

Characteristic: _____

_____

Notes: _____

_____

Reference: _____

_____

7sus2

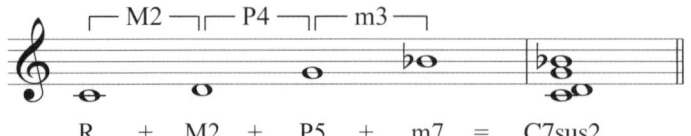

Characteristic: _____

_____

Notes: _____

_____

Reference: _____

_____

 TRACK 185 Sus 7 Chords Listening Exercise

SEVENTH CHORD INVERSIONS

Don't forget to practice your ear training with the different inversions of the seventh chords.

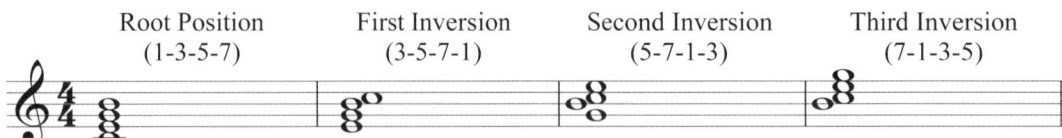

Root Position

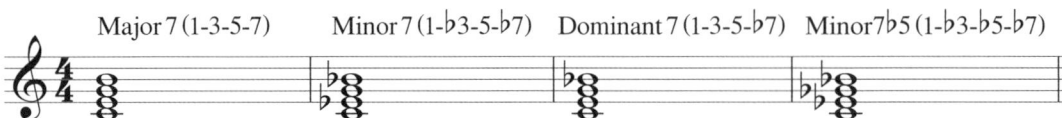

First Inversion

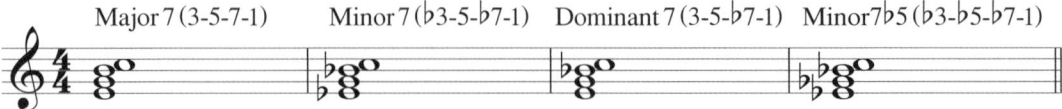

Second Inversion

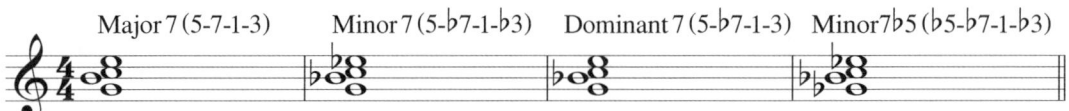

Third Inversion

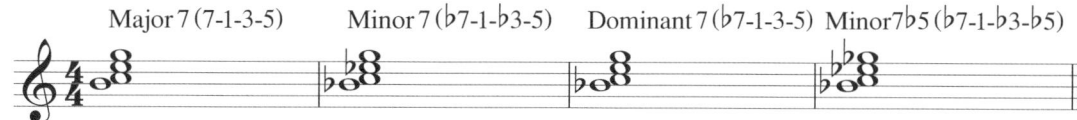

🔊 **TRACK 186** Major 7 Chord Inversion Listening Exercise

🔊 **TRACK 187** Minor 7 Chord Inversion Listening Exercise

🔊 **TRACK 188** Dominant 7 Chord Inversion Listening Exercise

🔊 **TRACK 189** Minor 7b5 Chord Inversion Listening Exercise

SEVENTH CHORD PROGRESSIONS

The seven seventh chords below are based on the diatonic major scale. Like triads, each interval of the major scale has a corresponding chord. If we are in a major key, the chords used in that key are built from each interval of the major scale. This is how you can connect the dots in music. On the bandstand, a key can be mentioned and a musician will know which notes are in that key and which chords correspond to each note.

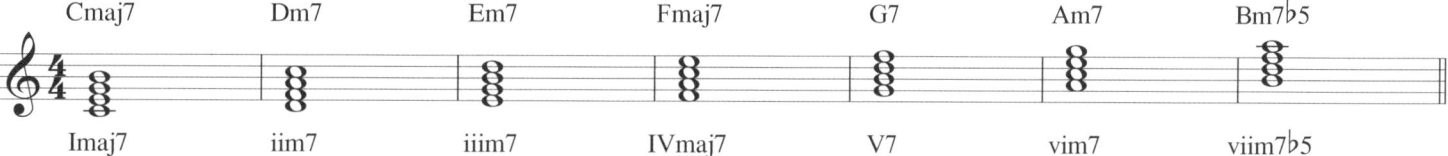

Roman numerals are used to represent the degrees (intervals) of the major scale and the chord quality of each chord. Uppercase roman numerals are used for major chords and lowercase numerals are used for minor chords.

Major Key Chord Sequence

SCALE/CHORD DEGREE	UPPERCASE ROMAN NUMERAL	LOWERCASE ROMAN NUMERAL	TRIAD	SEVENTH CHORD
1	I	i	I major	I major 7
2	II	ii	ii minor	ii minor 7
3	III	iii	iii minor	iii minor 7
4	IV	iv	IV major	IV major 7
5	V	v	V major	V dominant 7
6	VI	vi	iii minor	iii minor 7
7	VII	vii	vii diminished	vii minor 7b5

FOLLOW THE CHORD SEQUENCE

I had you do an exercise called "Follow the Root" at the end of Chapter 7. That exercise was a warm-up for this exercise. Practice playing through the chord sequence of the major scale. Start with triads and move on to seventh chords. This is a great way to familiarize yourself with the sound of major key chords and how they relate to each other.

CHAPTER 11:
Rhythm

FEELING RHYTHM

It's time; do you feel it? On the bandstand, the word "feel" is used to describe the rhythm that will be played. We want to feel the groove and vibe of the song we are playing. We feel a part of a band and we play off the feel or energy of the crowd. There is a lot of feeling going on, both physical sensations and emotion. Whatever you may discern from all of the feeling, it's something we are looking to be part of. Whenever you tap your foot, nod your head, or shift your body in time with a rhythm, you are not just hearing, you are hearing and feeling. Being able to feel and identify rhythm is part of ear training. You are training yourself to know and feel particular rhythm durations, identify different meters, and essentially intuit all things rhythm related. Rhythm is mathematical due to it dealing with time and duration. In the next few chapters, we will break down rhythm in its simplest forms, work on understanding and building rhythmic vocabulary, and how to practice and evolve our personal relationship with rhythm.

> *"There is music wherever there is rhythm, as there is life wherever there beats a pulse."*
> —*Igor Stravinsky*

RHYTHM OVERVIEW

Notes and rests have specific values—in other words, *durations* or *lengths*. The difference between quarter notes and eighth notes is the addition of a "flag" attached to the stem. Shorter durations are written by adding a flag, which indicates a halving of the value. An eighth note has one flag, a sixteenth note has two flags, and so on. Notice how the same theme applies to rests.

The duration of these note and rest values are proportional to one another.

NAME	NOTE	VALUE (no. of beats)	REST	NAME
whole note	𝅝	4	𝄻	whole rest
half note	𝅗𝅥 𝅗𝅥	2	𝄼 𝄼	half rest
quarter note	𝅘𝅥 𝅘𝅥 𝅘𝅥 𝅘𝅥	1	𝄽 𝄽 𝄽 𝄽	quarter rest
eighth note	𝅘𝅥𝅮 𝅘𝅥𝅮 𝅘𝅥𝅮 𝅘𝅥𝅮 𝅘𝅥𝅮 𝅘𝅥𝅮 𝅘𝅥𝅮 𝅘𝅥𝅮	1/2	𝄾 𝄾 𝄾 𝄾 𝄾 𝄾 𝄾 𝄾	eighth rest
sixteenth note	𝅘𝅥𝅯×16	1/4	𝄿×16	sixteenth rest

Dotted rhythms are equal to one and a half times the value of the normal note or rest.

NAME	NOTE	REST	VALUE (no. of beats)
Dotted whole note/rest	𝒐.	▬.	6
Dotted half note/rest	♩.	▬.	3
Dotted quarter note/rest	♩.	𝄽.	1 1/2
Dotted eighth note/rest	♪.	𝄾.	3/4
Dotted sixteenth note/rest	♬.	𝄿.	3/8

A *tie* is another way to increase the duration of a note. A tie is a curved line connecting two notes. The duration of the tied notes is equal to the notes being tied. Ties are used when a note is held over a bar line or in place of a dot to make the strong beats in a measure clearer.

Notes with *flags* are often *beamed* when appearing in groups of two or four. One beam for eighth notes, and two beams for sixteenth notes.

RHYTHM COMPONENTS

Rhythm, from the Greek word "rhythmos," is any recurring motion. Rhythm is a movement marked by the regulated succession of strong and weak elements. With rhythm, we look for symmetry, repeatable patterns that we can connect with, and an organization of silence and sound. Within this organization, we find the *beat*, align to the *tempo*, and notice any *accents* that make the rhythm unique or familiar.

Beat
Beat is a regular occurring pulse that underlies a piece of music. Like the tick-tock of a clock, beat is inherent in each musical phrase. When you tap your foot to music, you do it at a steady pace; this is the beat.

Tempo
Tempo is the speed and flow of a musical idea measured in bpm (beats per minute). Devices like a metronome are used to track the beat and set the tempo. It is important to align your personal rhythm to the beat and tempo when playing with others or with a metronome.

Accent
Accent is any emphasis given to a rhythm or note. This can be related to volume, length, or tone.

TIME SIGNATURE

At the beginning of a piece of music, a *time signature* denotes how many beats are in a measure and what type of note gets one beat. In 4/4 time, each measure has four beats (top number), and the quarter note (bottom number) is the type of note that gets the beat. Here are some examples:

Common and Cut Time

4/4 time is called *common time* and will frequently be seen with a 𝄴 in place of the numerical time signature. 2/2 is called *cut time* and the symbol used is a 𝄵. The sum of each measure is the same in duration (four quarter notes are equal to two half notes), and the difference is in how the meter is perceived and performed. Cut time is generally faster in tempo and the meter "feels" clearly like two beats, hence cut time, cutting four in half.

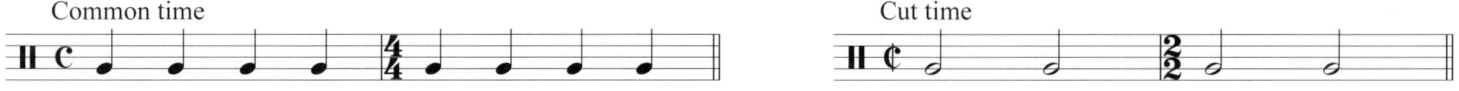

THE COUNT

The initial step when working with rhythm is to count the beats in each measure at tempo. In most cases, a count based on the time signature is used. For example: If we are in 4/4 time, we'd count each beat as 1, 2, 3, 4 and repeat that count for each measure. In 3/4 time, we'd use a count of 1, 2, 3 for each measure. Each beat can be broken down into fractions based on the meter or rhythm being used. In 4/4 time, quarter notes are counted just like we count the beat: 1, 2, 3, 4.

Eighth notes being half of a beat are counted using "&" between the beats. 1&, 2&, 3&, 4&.

1 & 2 & 3 & 4 &

Sixteenth notes being a quarter of a beat are counted using an "e" (pronounced 'ee') and "a" (pronounced 'ah') between the divisions. We'd count a measure of sixteenths as 1e&a, 2e&a, 3e&a, 4e&a.

1 e & a 2 e & a 3 e & a 4 e & a

When rhythms arise, count each rhythm along with the beat based on the lowest common denominator for that beat.

1 & 2 e & a 3 & 4 e & a   1 e & a 2 e & a 3 e & a 4 e & a

1 e & a 2 e & a 3 e & a 4   &   1 e & a 2 e & a 3 e & a 4

METER

Meter is the word used to describe how the basic beats are grouped and divided. There are two types of meter: *simple meter* and *compound meter*. Simple meter is when the beats of a musical passage are divided into subdivisions of two. Compound meter is when the beats are divided into subdivisions of three.

Simple Duple

Simple Triple

Simple Quadruple

69

Compound Duple

Compound Triple

Compound Quadruple

RHYTHM SYSTEMS

The count or number system is the standard Western practice for reading and counting rhythms. There are also other rhythm systems using different syllables or sounds instead of a count. Systems like "Takadimi" are great for internalizing a rhythm as a sound, much like singing. When it comes to learning, using your voice is the best conduit for the integration of music. The goal is to internalize the rhythm; count until it becomes a knowing, so when you see a particular rhythm, you know how it sounds. Use sounds like da, da, da, or ti, ti, ti, or de, de, de, etc. Channel the inner kid and make some noise. I counted and later started singing the rhythms in my own way until I knew how each rhythm felt in time. At times, I will count when my nerves get the best of me on a gig. Having a foundational system to fall back on is essential. The different rhythm systems don't all function the same way the number system does, but you may find them interesting and/or useful nonetheless.

Konnakol/Takadimi

♩ (half)	=	ta-ah
♩ (quarter)	=	ta
♫ (two eighths)	=	ta di
♬ (four sixteenths)	=	taka dimi

French Time-Names

♩ (half)	=	ta-ah
♩ (quarter)	=	ta
♫ (two eighths)	=	ta te
♬ (four sixteenths)	=	tafa tefe

Kodály

♩ (half)	=	ta-ah or too-oo
♩ (quarter)	=	ta
♫ (two eighths)	=	ti ti
♬ (four sixteenths)	=	tiri tiri or tika tika

Gordon

♩ (half)	=	du-u
♩ (quarter)	=	du
♫ (two eighths)	=	du de
♬ (four sixteenths)	=	duta deta

Solfeggio

𝅗𝅥	=	too
♩	=	ta
♫	=	ti ti
♬	=	tika tika

Strong and Weak Beats

In a piece of music, some beats are more important than others. We differentiate these beats by calling them *strong* and *weak beats*. You've probably heard the term *downbeat*, which is the first beat in a measure. The downbeat is a strong beat, and a general rule is that the first beat (downbeat) is always going to be strong. Another word you've most likely heard is *upbeat*, which describes the weak beats in between the strong beats. Picture in your mind a conductor waving a baton to start a piece of music. Each downward motion sets the pulse, while the upward motion keeps the flow of time. Consider a hi-hat on a drum kit. When playing a simple drum beat, the hi-hat plays with the kick and snare on the strong beats and on the weak beats in-between.

S = Strong beat
W = Weak beat

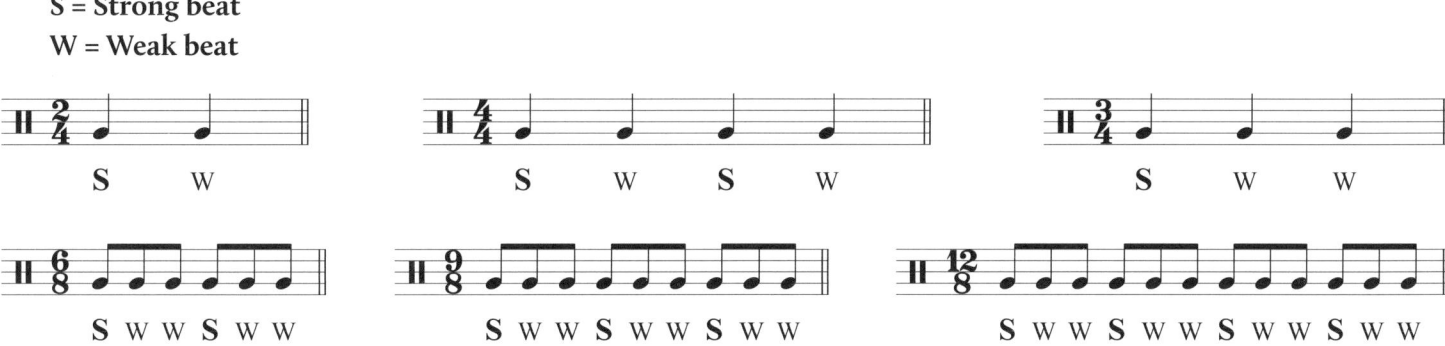

TRIPLETS

A *triplet* is when a beat being divided by two is temporarily divided by three. Another way to think of a triplet is as a temporary shift to compound meter. We write a triplet by adding the number 3 above a bracket of three notes.

Sixteenth note triplet	♬³ is equal to ♫	1/2 beat
Eighth note triplet	♪♪♪³ is equal to ♫	1 beat
Quarter note triplet	♩♩♩³ is equal to ♩♩	2 beats
Half note triplet	𝅗𝅥𝅗𝅥𝅗𝅥³ is equal to 𝅗𝅥𝅗𝅥	4 beats

Triplet Count

A triplet can be counted in a few different ways. With a temporary shift to compound meter (subdivisions of three), counting a triplet can be awkward at first. As you can see in the example below, there's a measure of 4/4 and the second half of the measure has two triplets. It's really like a measure of 2/4 to a measure of 6/8. If we counted the same measure in the compound time 12/8, the first two beats are dotted quarter notes (the quarter notes being subdivisions of three).

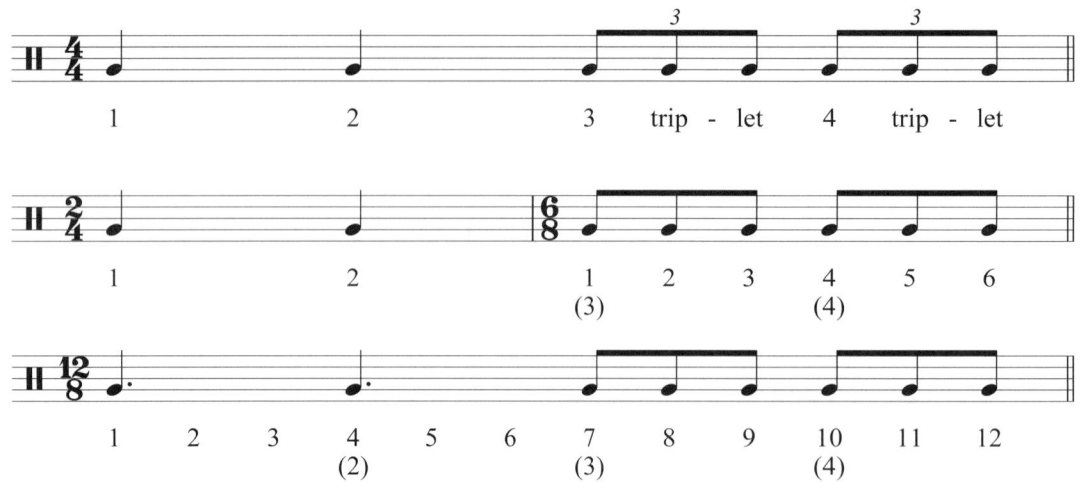

How you count a triplet using the number system is, fortunately or unfortunately, up to you (depending on how you look at it). Choose a way to count triplets and stick with it. Below are four options that are commonly used:

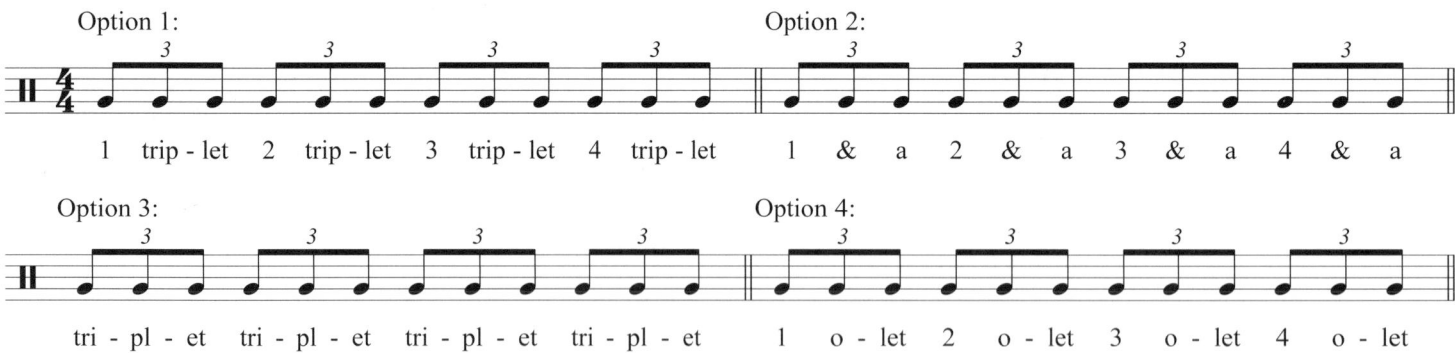

Triplet Variations

Music won't always be three notes when subdividing in groups of three. Here are some common triplet patterns adding a rest in place of a note or grouping two of the three notes together.

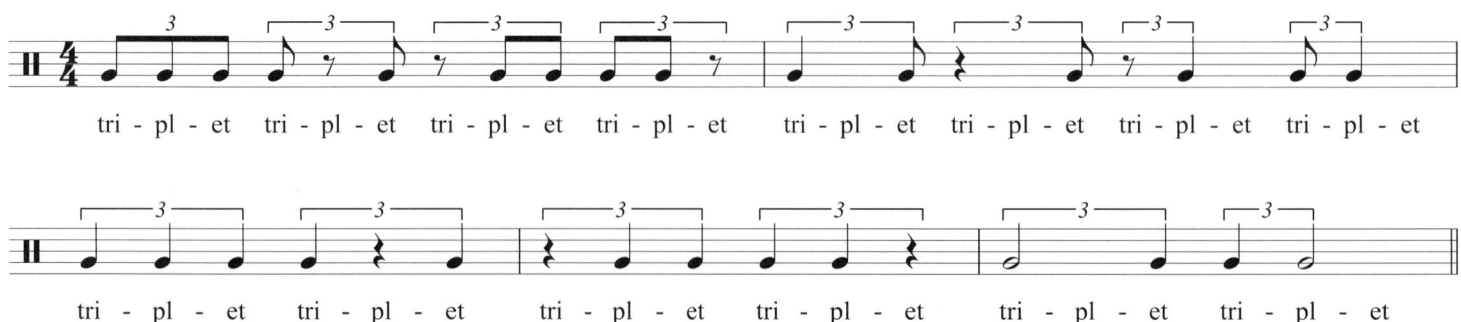

SHUFFLE/SWING FEEL

A *shuffle* or *swing feel* is an eighth note feel based on triplets rather than subdivisions of two. It's written in simple meter, but instead of writing out triplets for every beat, a note is made stating: "shuffle" or "swing," indicating that even though it's written in simple meter, it's felt in compound meter (subdivisions of three). A shuffle rhythm ties the first two notes of a triplet, making them one, and the third note of the triplet is the second note. In the example below, all three measures sound the same even though they are notated differently.

Swing Exercise

Swing is a very common rhythmic feel. It's Jazz to the core, we even call Jazz "Swing." It don't mean a thing … you know what I mean? The fact that most swing music is usually written with standard rhythms can make it difficult to learn. The global instruction to play in a swing feel at the top of a chart can be overlooked. Swing feel is a big deal, rhythmically speaking, it makes or breaks certain feels and styles. Dig into this exercise if you want to work on your swing feel. Practice the rhythm only at first, or if you add pitch, keep it to one note.

1. Start by playing straight eighths on an instrument. Use percussive elements like muted (dead) notes on a stringed instrument or a single pitch. You could clap or tap as well. Hum or make a noise using your voice along with whatever you are playing.
2. Gradually turn the eighths into triplets. Double the first note when playing melodic passages.
3. Remove the middle note of the triplet and accent the first note a little. Hold the first note all the way through to the second note.

TRACK 190 Swing Groove

You can do this exercise using any eight-note melodic line. Use a C major scale for practice.

 TRACK 191 Swing Scale

CHAPTER 12:
Time Elements

Our relationship to time and tempo is an essential part of ear training, listening, and playing music. In this chapter, we'll look at different time elements and ways to improve our ability to hear and feel time.

TEMPO SENSE

Recalling or having a good sense of tempo based on tempo markings or remembering the tempo of a song you're going to play is a skill that can be acquired and improved upon. Ask any drummer how important tempo is when having to count off a night's worth of music. It can be a challenge to remember and get tempos correct. A good start when working on tempo is to memorize the standard tempo marking names and ranges. If you want to work on tempo itself, a good practice is to take a tempo and be able to cut it in half or double it effectively (within a natural range).

Keeping Time Exercise

An essential skill as a musician is our ability to play in time. Building an internal clock is not a drummers-only skill, it's part of being a musician. Just like improving our ability to recognize pitches, playing in time is equally important. We have an innate timing advantage that we often don't consider; our ability to vocalize. In conversation, we naturally speak with a cadence. Even when counting, we naturally fall into a rhythm where the words are generally equally spaced. Test yourself now by counting aloud from 1 to 4. Do it again, counting slower. Did you notice the timing being regular? Practice counting when you play an instrument. Being able to count and play helps your natural time and feel. Let me repeat myself, practice counting when you play an instrument.

A great way to work on building your internal clock is to play along with music, grooves, or a metronome for several measures, have the music drop out for two or four measures, and come back in while you continue to play. When the music comes back in, what do you notice most often? Three possibilities arise:

- Are you on time and in sync?
- Do you push or play on top of the time?
- Did you lag or play behind the time?

Practice this time-keeping exercise often over the next few weeks to see if you can adjust in any direction. Record yourself and listen to your timing. Do you push or pull when playing music? What you are looking for is the ability to play all three ways! First, you want to stay in sync with time. Keep your place. It's okay to push or pull as long as you don't drop time. Most musicians tend to play with time almost like their personality. If you are laid back, most likely you played laid-back and so on. The ability to push or pull on demand comes with practice. For some music, a push creates drive and anticipation. While the ability to lag behind is what some musicians strive for. A laid-back, "behind the time" feel can be the grooviest feel of all. This is a helpful timing exercise to make part of your practice regime.

Here are four examples of grooves at different tempos that drop out and come back in. Each example will start off with an 8-bar groove pattern for you to lock in with. After the 8 bars, the pattern will drop out and the drum groove will continue for another 32 measures. Jam along with the drums, keep time, and have fun. The drums will drop out at different locations. Keep time and notice if you're still in the pocket when the drums come back in. When the drums drop out, are you able to keep time and make the dropouts seamless? If your time gets off, see if you can notice whether you push or pull.

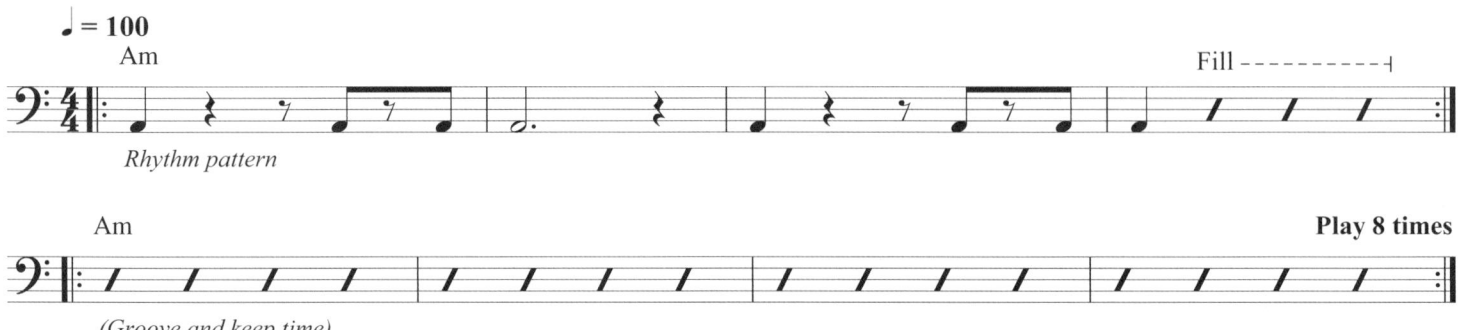

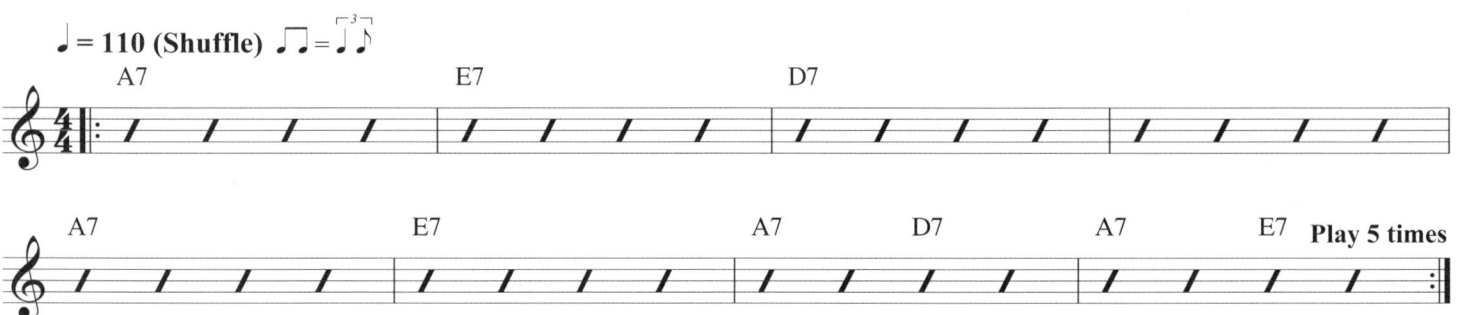

76

SHIFTING TIME AND METER

Let's demystify time signatures. This is a listening exercise to hear how time signatures and meter work. This exercise requires participation. The audio examples will be played two times. Follow the directions and do the exercise. Most often what we think we can do, isn't actually what we can do. Test yourself.

In this example, notice the shift to different time signatures does not change tempo or fluctuate anything other than the meter subdivisions being multiples of two or three. It'll shift time signatures almost every measure toward the end.

1. Listen: I'll count aloud whenever a time signature changes.

2. Exercise: Keep the quarter note pulse with your foot and tap the rhythms with your hands.

🔊 **TRACK 196** 2/4, 6/8, 4/4, and 12/8

Odd Time Signatures

Now that you are familiar with the most common time signatures, let's add a few uncommon time signatures to help embed the idea of time signatures in your mind and ears. With the next two examples, we are changing the number of beats in a measure. We call uncommon time signatures "odd" time signatures due to our propensity to generally work in multiples of two. Even when we are working in multiples of three, we tend to group in even numbers; 2 threes, 4 threes, and so on. Odd numbers can feel like a skip at first until the pattern becomes familiar. Drum grooves will play throughout each example. Drum patterns over odd time signatures have common patterns in which they accent the beat and can help you hear and feel odd time signatures. Each example will be played twice; follow the directions below:

1. Listen: I'll count aloud the first time through so you can follow along.

2. Exercise: Keep the pulse with your foot and count aloud.

3. Exercise: Play through each example with an instrument. Start with playing quarter notes (any key) and move into eighth notes.

TRACK 197 Odd Quarters

We start out in 4/4 time and move into 5/4. 5/4 can feel like 4/4 with one beat added due to the snare generally landing on beat 5 (but not always). It's two measures of 5/4, then back to 4/4 to help balance out the quirk you might feel, followed by two measures of 3/4. In 3/4, the snare generally lands on beat 3 to accent time in a three feel. Next are two bars of 6/4, which can feel like a bar of 4/4 plus 2/4 because the snare will generally land on beats 4 and 6. Note: If you want the pulse to stay in a three feel, you'd use 3/4, not 6/4.

Now something new: two measures of 7/4 and then back to 4/4. 7/4 is a little more open with its accents on the snare drum. 7/4 time can feel like 6/4 with an added beat (snare on beats 2 and 4) or like two bars of 3/4 (snare on beats 3) with an added beat. In 7/4, the snare will often land on upbeats. In this example, the snare lands on beats 3, 5&, and 7. Knowing where accents land on rhythm parts will help you stay in the pocket when playing music with others. It is uncommon to switch time signatures this often in a piece of music—unless you're in a progressive rock band like "Animals as Leaders," "Tool," or "Rush"—with that said, keep in mind this is an exercise to help demystify odd times.

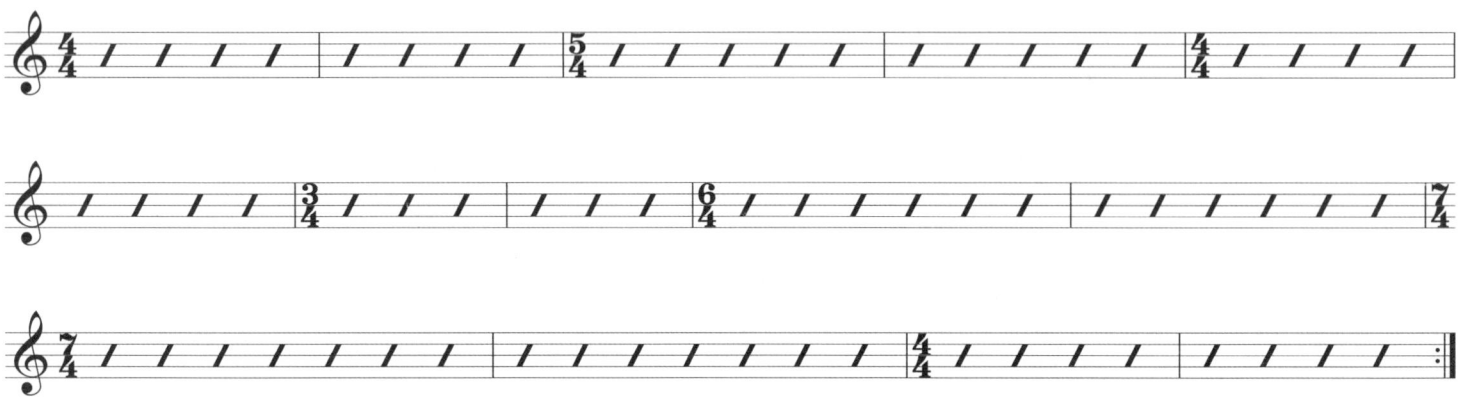

TRACK 198 Odd Eighths

Following the theme of the last example, we will work with odd times in a compound meter. We start out with four bars of 6/8, which is a common feel used a lot due to its inherent swing and move into four bars of 5/8. 5/8 feels almost exactly like 6/8 but with one beat dropped.

We use two bars of 3/8 as a transition into four bars of 7/8. In this instance of 3/8, the snare accent is on beat 3, which sets up the feel of 7/8 that is accenting the snare on beats 3 and 7. Lastly, we play two bars of 12/8, which switches the snare accents back to beats 4 and 10, very similar to 4/4 with a triplet feel. Actually, exactly like 4/4 with a triplet feel. Working with an eighth-note pulse can help break us out of the tendency to group things into even numbers.

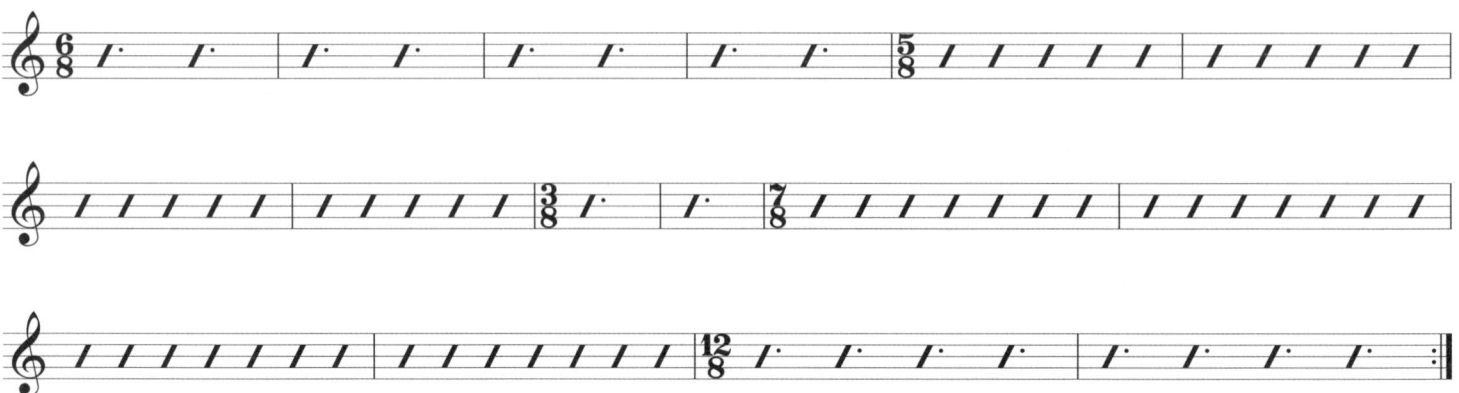

Odd Time Practice Tips

How do you become familiar with odd time signatures? Find an odd time reference, a song or example that you are familiar with. Play, practice, and compose. It's an action item. Here are suggestions for practice if you'd like to go farther down the road of odd time signatures.

1. Start counting the time signatures of songs you listen to. Find songs in odd time signatures.
2. Practice with drum grooves in odd times. Set up a loop and groove with your instrument or set up a click and play drums or percussion until what you're practicing feels natural.
3. Compose an *ostinato* in the time signature you want to master. An ostinato is a motif or phrase that persistently repeats. The bassline for "Money" from Pink Floyd is a great example of an ostinato bass part in 7/4 time.
4. Look for cover songs (a reference) in odd time signatures. Learn the songs and play along until it feels natural.
5. Take notes and break things down into smaller chunks. How do you feel it? Does 5/4 feel like a measure of 3/4 and 2/4? Does 7/4 feel like a measure of 4/4 and 3/4? Work with what is already familiar and build from that.

METRONOME USE

A metronome or click track is used to set the beat of music when recording and practicing. As a practice tool, a metronome sets the beat and the musical time, and we synchronize our personal time to that musical time. We all have our own internal musical time; you can liken it to your personal walk. When we play music with others, it's like walking together, we match pace. Great bands can flow and groove together like birds in a flock, all synchronized to the musical time, in the moment. When you practice using a metronome, you are practicing this synchronization skill.

A metronome is great for reading notation. It helps you stay on track as if you are in a performance. If you make the same mistake in the same section repeatedly, stop the metronome, learn the rhythm, and continue.

If playing to a metronome is difficult, a few things may be happening. Below are some scenarios and suggestions that may help if you have a hard time playing to a metronome:

- I've seen students have a hard time continuing to listen to the metronome when playing. They get lost in their own time feel, so much so that the metronome beat is lost to them. This can happen often when learning new material. Practice playing familiar material with a metronome until it becomes natural.
- Listening to yourself play and the metronome gets "tuned out." Playing over the metronome not with it. Stop and practice interacting by hearing yourself play and try to connect and play with the metronome, not over it. Count aloud with it.
- Syncing can be hard if you are not feeling the beat. The beat is a physical thing, and you want to feel it in your body. Hum it if you need to connect to the beat. Tap or sway with the beat.
- Distraction is a big one. As we practice, our mind wanders to thoughts and images of whatever is up in our lives. Bring your mind back by getting into your body and feeling the beat. Focus your attention on the metronome and imagine expanding the beat like it's a kick drum or another percussion instrument. Use your mind to expand it into other rhythms. Be creative, and you'll be thinking and feeling music.

Metronomes are widely available at no cost. They are online, and if you have a phone or tablet, you can download an app.

 TRACK 199 Metronome Exercise

Working with a metronome or click track is an essential skill. It improves your ability to play in time with others. It helps improve your internal timing and sense of tempo. It's fun to play with a metronome, to groove with it. With technology in all areas being a common part of the musical world, being proficient with a metronome is a must. Recording audio, video, live performance, practicing at home, it all has been infiltrated with the metronome. You'll spend more energy avoiding a metronome than you will learning how to play with one. It will, most likely, come ticking on your door. Best be prepared. Here are six ways to work with a metronome.

Normal Click
A metronome is usually set up to play one click for every beat. If the quarter note gets the beat, then the click is played in quarter notes. If the eighth note gets the beat, then the click usually plays in eighth notes. This is the standard way to set up a metronome or click.

Double Time Click
A metronome set to play at each beat isn't always ideal. If the tempo is slow, the rhythm you are playing is intricate, or if you think more subdivisions will help your timing or groove; double the metronome. If it's set at quarter notes, set it to eighths instead.

Subdivision Click
Set the click to play the smallest subdivision you are playing. If you're playing a tight sixteenth pattern, click at sixteenths. An eighth-note rock drive, try the click at eighths. Set the click to a triplet feel if you are playing a shuffle.

Half Time Click (Beats 1 & 3)
Breaking up the click is great for your rhythm. Having the click on beats one and three is much like a kick drum pattern.

Half Time Click (Beats 2 & 4)
Playing with a click on two and four is great practice for a swing feel. It replicates the hi-hat playing on beats two and four. It can be tricky not having a click on the downbeat. Count aloud to orientate yourself if you need a downbeat.

Click on One
This is a great practice to work on timing. It's easier at fast tempos. At slow tempos, it can test your ability to keep time. Counting aloud while playing your instrument is helpful on this one.

EQUAL RHYTHMS

Rhythm and mathematics go hand in hand because we are dealing with subdivisions of time. Changing the tempo creates a shift in how we subdivide the beat. A quarter note at 200 bpm (beats per minute) feels the same as an eighth note at 100 bpm and a sixteenth note at 50 bpm. This may help you see the relationship between tempo and rhythm. Below are several rhythms that are all the same, but the tempo is cut in half each time it's written. If you cut the time in half, the measures are cut in half as well. This relationship between time and rhythm is helpful to see and understand, especially when transcribing and sight reading music. Familiarize yourself with the rhythms in this example; how to count them, how they sound, and how they feel. If you are having difficulty learning any eighth or sixteenth-note rhythm, you can apply this concept and break down any rhythm to something more basic.

Look at the example below and listen to the audio example played at 200, 100, and 50 beats per minute. Each example will have a count-in at the tempo changes, and a hi-hat will play the beats while a piano plays the rhythm.

 TRACK 200 Equal Rhythms 1

TRACK 201 Equal Rhythms 2

TRACK 202 Equal Rhythms 3

TRACK 203 Equal Rhythms 4

RHYTHM AND COUNT PRACTICE

Practicing rhythm without pitch is a great way to focus on your internal rhythm. A common recommendation made by countless great musicians is: In addition to a main instrument, being able to play drums or percussion adds invaluable skill to your musicianship. To focus on an instrument that is purely about time and groove can only help your feel and that translates everywhere, musically speaking. It's not a requirement if you play music, only a suggestion. You can practice rhythm on any instrument; clapping your hands or tapping on a table is another way to express and practice timing. Having a relationship with rhythm is the goal. Practice counting the beats aloud and play the rhythms by clapping, tapping on a table, or using a percussion instrument. Play through each exercise by yourself with a metronome and check yourself with the supplied track.

 TRACK 204 Rhythm and Count 1

 TRACK 205 Rhythm and Count 2

 TRACK 206 Rhythm and Count 3

 **TRACK 207** Rhythm and Count 4

GENRE

Genre, or *style*, is an expressive feel of music. It is often a reflection of culture and mimics the time and space in which it was created. One can mention a genre, and people will understand the sound and feel, much like the description of a person. Most genres are defined by a few specific rhythm patterns. We categorize music into styles to help identify the characteristics and rhythms we enjoy or relate to.

GROOVE

Groove can be likened to the gait of a walk, the style in which a person carries themselves. Movement carries a "vibe," and in music, groove is an individual's personal stamp. Every style or genre has a feel, but the groove of that style will generally depend on an individual's unique expression.

> *"Imitation is not just the sincerest form of flattery—it's the sincerest form of learning."*
> —*George Bernard Shaw*

CHAPTER 13:
Rhythm Dictation

THE VISUAL GRID

A common way to work with rhythm using modern technology is by using a *grid*. A grid looks much like a ruler and its scale is set to M:B:T, measures, beats, and ticks. Ticks are the mathematical division of each beat. A beat is equal to 960 ticks and each note length has a specific value. Sixteenth notes are 240 ticks, eighth notes 480, eighth note triplets 320, etc. Measure one, beat 1 would look like 1:01:000, measure three, beat 3& would be 3:03:480. This is commonplace in DAWs (digital audio workstations), drum machines, and synthesizers.

Most modern music is played with a click to enable the use of a grid. It creates ease when editing, sharing tracks, and working with different synthesizers and loops. If you don't know a rhythm, you can look at where a note lands on the grid (if played in time) and do the calculation. The example below is a staff with the M:B:T location placed above each note. This is only a reference to visualize what the readout would be if we stopped at each note.

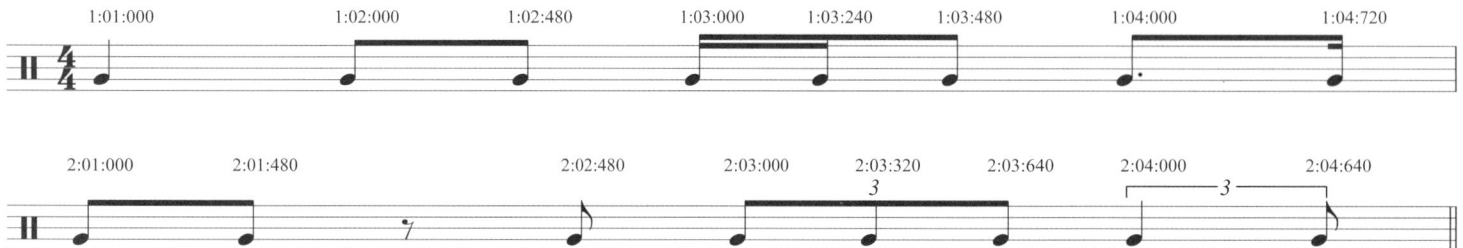

The images below show a M:B:T readout in different DAWs. The M:B:T readout is most commonly found at the top of your editing window.

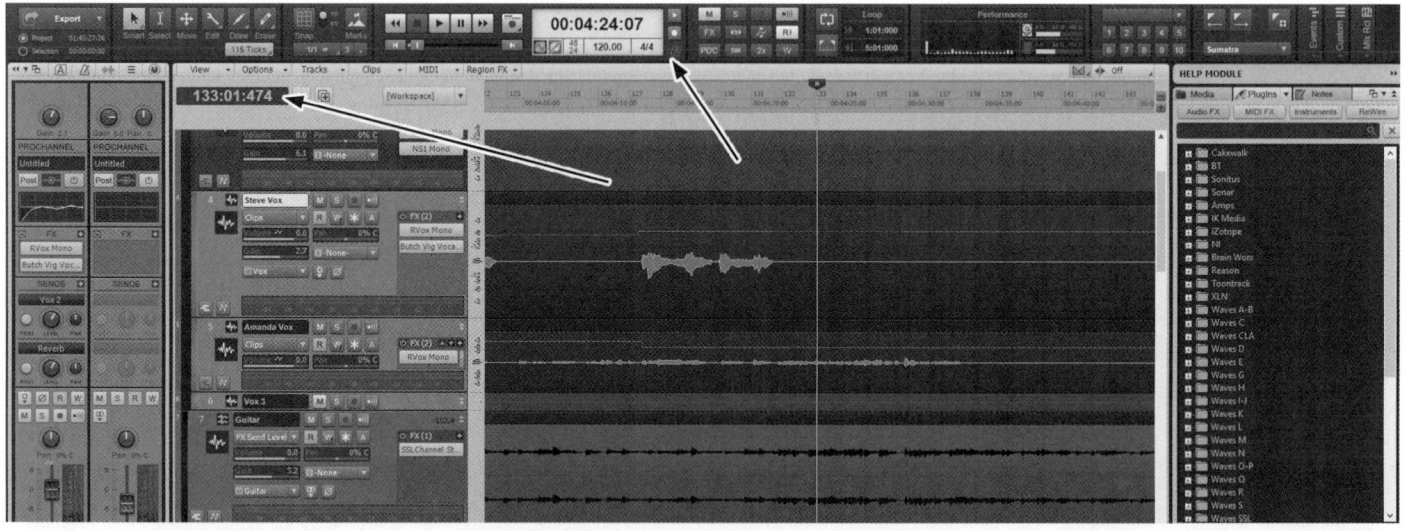

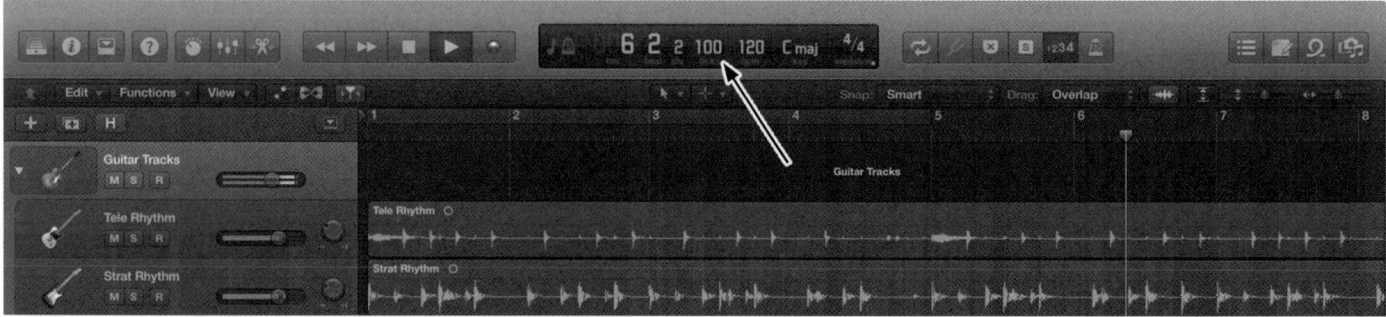

84

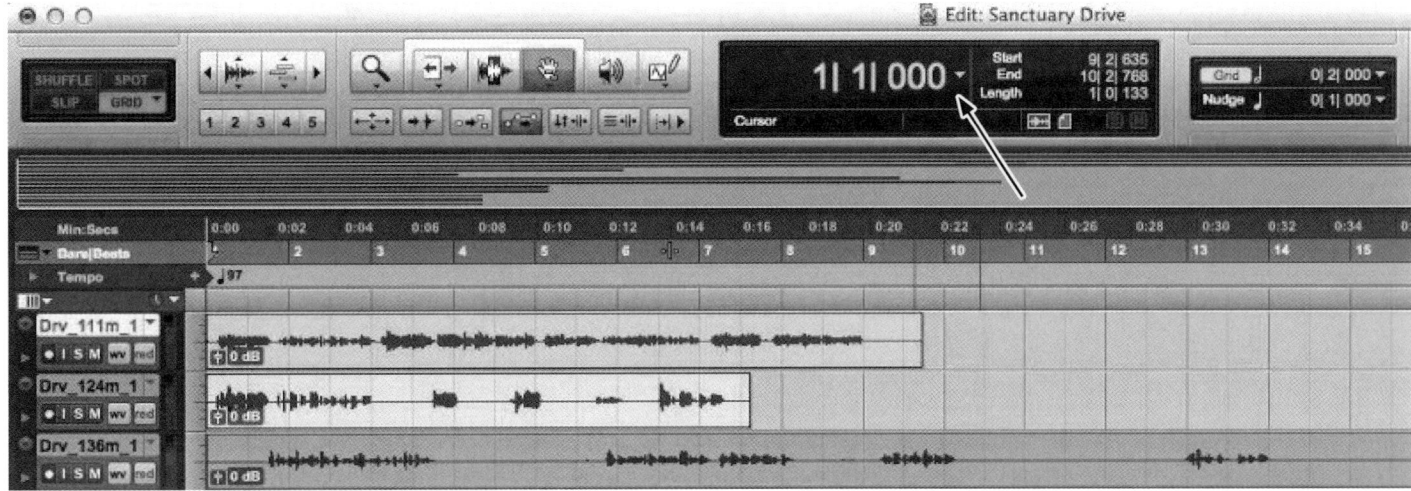

The grid is used as a template for editing and location in modern technology. It is a great tool to use as a visual representation of a measure of music. Below is an example of a drum machine grid, which represents one measure subdivided into sixteenth notes, four boxes, sometimes called steps, per beat. When a note is played, it is highlighted in the grid.

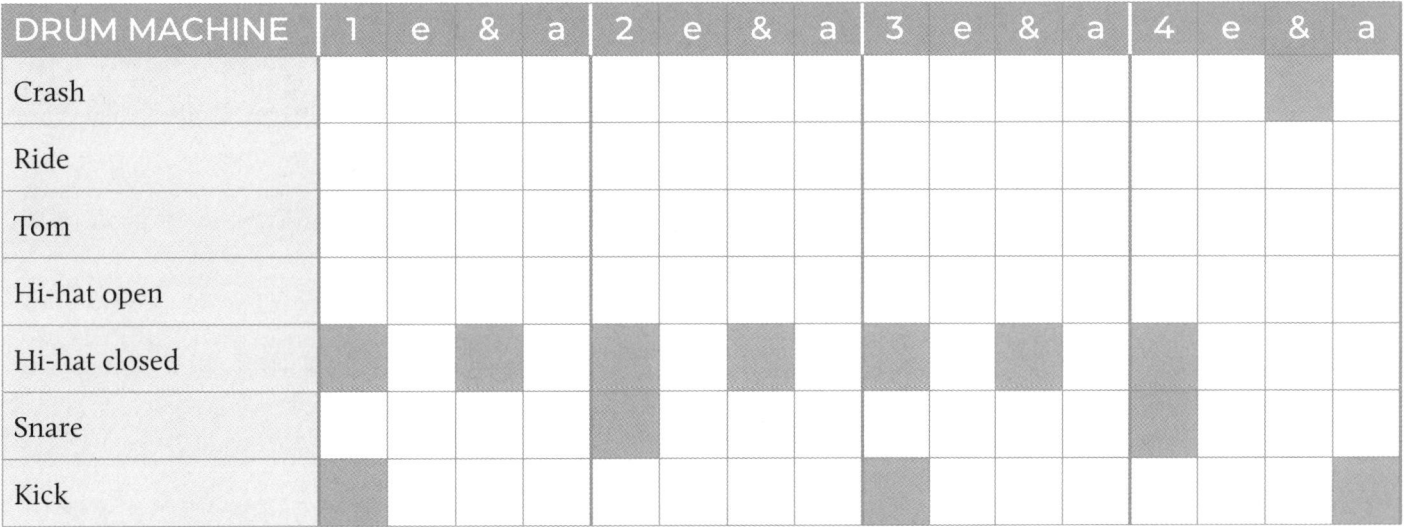

Here is the measure written in standard drum notation to reflect what's going on in the grid.

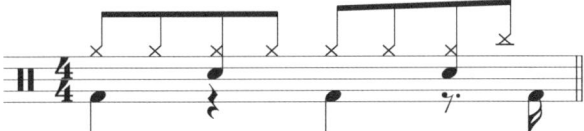

Here is an example of a "timeline" in two different windows of a DAW. Why is this helpful? Consider a map like this as a way to break up rhythms in your mind, especially where beats land in a measure.

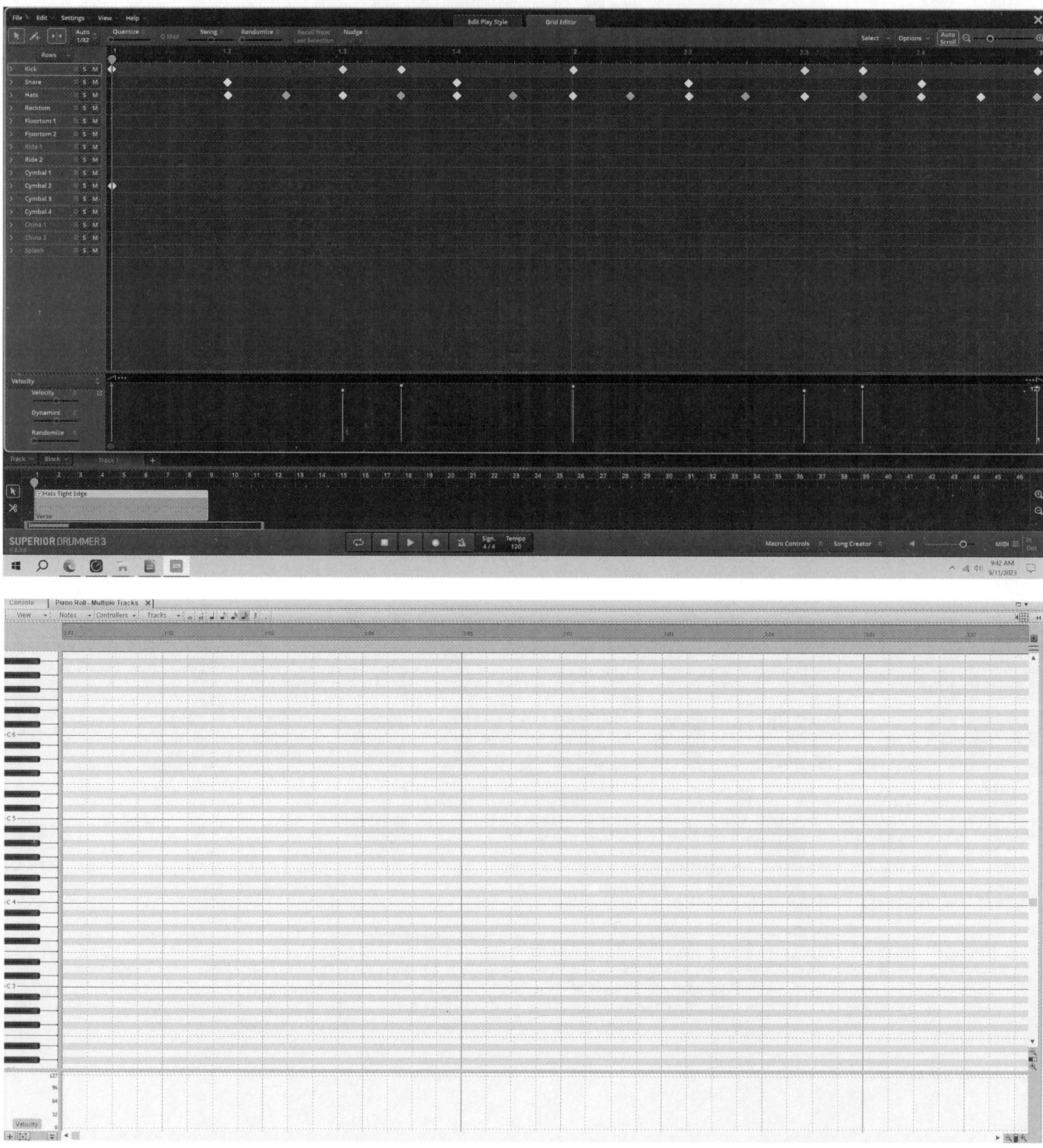

RHYTHMIC SUBDIVISIONS

Breaking rhythms into subdivisions helps with feel and timing. In the recording studio, it is common practice to subdivide the click when timing issues occur while recording. Changing a quarter-note click into an eighth-note click is an external way to help many musicians get the best take. How do we internalize and feel this subdivision? Practice. Feeling the subdivision of every beat enables fluidity and confidence within the measure, not only on the downbeat. A great way to internalize different rhythms is by practicing the subdivisions until it becomes an internal feeling.

Subdivision Exercise

Practice the rhythms in this exercise by either clapping or using your instrument. The use of a metronome is encouraged. I'll leave it up to you to find a creative way to implement the exercise on your instrument. The Xs indicate muted notes; play them lightly, and then accent the regular note. If you are clapping, clap lightly when there's an X, and louder when there's a note. The point of the exercise is to clearly differentiate between the notes and muted notes.

Start with sixteenth notes. Focus on feeling the subdivisions. Go through each rhythm until it feels comfortable and fluid. Then, move on to the examples with rests and feel the subdivision internally without having to play (or clap) them.

Sixteenth Subdivision

Triplet subdivisions can be harder for some people to feel. If that's true for you, remember to think compound time (like you're in 12/8) if you need help getting into the triplet subdivision.

Triplet Subdivision

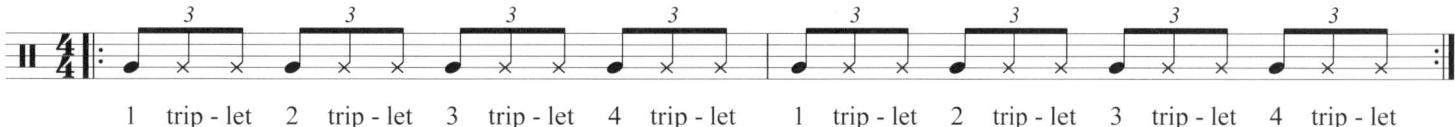

With music, it's important to go to new places, and maneuvering through different subdivisions takes you off the beaten path. Being comfortable working through different subdivisions increases your awareness and lowers your chances of getting lost when music goes off-road. Seriously, being able to feel rhythm and go to different places with confidence keeps your musical journey exciting. The subdivision exercise is a great way to practice internalizing rhythms. It's an exercise you can expand upon easily and create your own random patterns.

RHYTHM DICTATION

Rhythm dictation relies heavily on our ability to audiate or use our inner ear to recall what we hear. A rhythm is played, you listen and write the rhythm down. It's the same as transcribing; listening to a specific rhythm and accurately writing it down. With rhythmic dictation, we focus on note start times and durations. It is helpful to imagine a grid when writing rhythms out. Traditional rhythm dictation suggests beat marks above each measure to help with the process. One slash for each beat in the measure to help you mark where notes land in time before you write out the rhythms. Rhythm dictation is the traditional way to practice your rhythm knowledge.

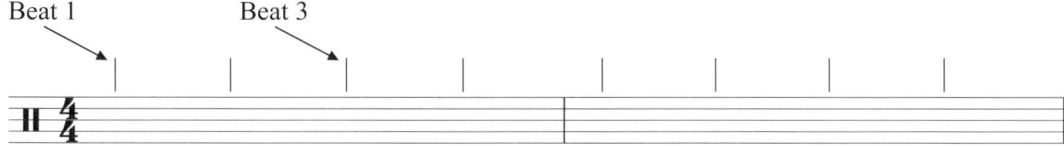

You can also use a visual grid for rhythm dictation like the examples below. Mark in the box when a note begins, and use an arrow horizontally to indicate note duration.

Eighth Note Grid (2 measures):

MEASURE 1								MEASURE 2							
1	&	2	&	3	&	4	&	1	&	2	&	3	&	4	&

Sixteenth Note Grid (2 measures):

There are an abundance of apps available for rhythm training and dictation. If you want a regular practice of rhythm dictation and other exercises, download an app and get started. With the internet, you have more information available to you than you can possibly keep up with. Find an app you like and **stick with it**. It's easy to get distracted looking for practice tools instead of actually practicing.

 Dictation Grids

Rhythm Dictation Exercise

Let's do some rhythm dictation. This is a brief introduction to get you started. Look for an app or a place online to continue your rhythmic development practice if you prefer dictation to other methods discussed in this book. Below are empty measures for each example with rhythm dictation marks to help when you transcribe. All indicated rhythms include rests of the same value.

1. Four measures of rhythm using a G note will be played. The quiz will repeat four times, including a count-in measure on each repeat.
2. Listen to the rhythm while counting along. Tap your foot with each beat.
3. Mark note start times using dictation marks (if needed) or a dictation grid.
4. Count note durations and write that down. Notice any rests.
5. Translate all markings into note values and complete.
6. Check your work one more time by playing along with the quiz.

Check your answers with the  Rhythm Quiz Answers.

🔊 **TRACK 208 Rhythm Quiz 1** (whole, half, quarter)

TRACK 209 Rhythm Quiz 2 (whole, half, quarter, eighth)

TRACK 210 Rhythm Quiz 3 (whole, half, quarter, eighth, including dotted notes and ties)

TRACK 211 Rhythm Quiz 4 (whole, half, quarter, eighth)

TRACK 212 Rhythm Quiz 5 (whole, half, quarter, eighth, sixteenth)

TRACK 213 Rhythm Quiz 6 (whole, half, quarter, eighth, sixteenth)

TRACK 214 Rhythm Quiz 7 (quarter, quarter-note triplet, eighth, eighth-note triplet)

TRACK 215 **Rhythm Quiz 8** (whole, half, quarter, eighth, eighth-note triplet, sixteenth)

TRACK 216 **Rhythm Quiz 9** (whole, half, quarter, quarter-note triplet, eighth, eighth-note triplet, sixteenth)

TRACK 217 **Rhythm Quiz 10** (whole, half, quarter, quarter-note triplet, eighth, eighth-note triplet, sixteenth)

CHAPTER 14:
Do-It-Yourself!

PLANTING SEEDS

Below are several topics for your exploration. In the "do-it-yourself" spirit, these topics are seeds I'm hoping to plant for you to water and evolve. We are at an unprecedented time at which all the world's information is at our fingertips. It's easy to take in too much information without focused discipline. Hopefully the practice tools from Chapter 3 will keep you focused and on track!

PITCH AND RHYTHM

Most of the rhythm exercises in this book deal strictly with rhythm and exclude pitch. In the do-it-yourself spirit; take the foundational concepts from this book and merge your pitch and rhythm exercises together. The best way to practice rhythm and pitch is by transcribing.

TRANSCRIPTION

Transcription is musical dictation, the skill of translating music and writing it into musical notation. This is an indispensable skill that evolves your ear and musical knowledge in every way. Keep in mind that transcription isn't easy; it falls into the "desirable difficulty" category. As mentioned before, working through some difficulty creates the best kind of learning, the type of learning that sticks. Transcription is, in my experience, the best way to practice ear training and the language of music in one exercise.

HEARING CHORD CHANGES

Hearing chord changes in a song starts with being able to track root note movement. Chapter 7 "Follow the Root" is a great practice to start you off. Once you can track the root movement, the second step is detecting the quality of each chord. Being able to sing your chords from root position is the most basic exercise and a good exercise to keep working on. We've covered the most common chords in this book, and hopefully, by this point, you can identify common chord sounds. Hearing chords is a work in progress, so don't get disheartened if you get stuck often. The more you do it, the easier it will become.

Working with guide tones is another common practice to explore. Guide tones are typically the 3rd and 7th scale degree of a chord. The 3rd and 7th scale degrees determine whether a chord is major, minor, or dominant. The 3rd is the most stable, and an obvious giveaway to whether a chord is major or minor. Guide tone lines are melodic lines constructed from tones that are built from a song's chord changes. Playing guide tone lines is a great practice when hearing chord progressions because you'll be studying how chord changes relate within a song.

SIGHT SINGING

Sight singing or melodic dictation is recognizing melodic phrases and singing or hearing in your head what you see on paper. An example of this would be if you were about to play a jazz tune and were able to hear the melody in your head just by looking at the written music. It can also include the ability to transcribe a melodic passage without an instrument. We delved into scale singing and broken intervals in Chapter 7. Sight singing is a continuation of that skill set. Remember to listen to each phrase before trying to figure out what's going on. Listen first.

CHORD EXTENSIONS/ALTERATIONS

Adding extensions or alterations to chords is an essential practice. When playing chords with extensions like 9ths, 11ths, and 13ths, sometimes it is physically impossible to include all the notes implied by the chord symbol. It is then up to the player to decide which notes in the chord to use. Notice in the third row of the table below, there is an augmented 2nd interval. Remember, when perfect intervals are increased by a half step, they become augmented—the same is true for major intervals. So, when a major 2nd is increased by a half step, it becomes an augmented 2nd (which is the same distance as a minor 3rd).

9	M2
♭9	m2
#9	A2 (m3)
11	P4
#11	A4 (tritone)
13	M6
♭13	m6

CHORD TYPES

Understand the different chord symbols and learn how the chords sound. A chord symbol is built starting with the root, then the chord quality (major, minor, etc.), then the highest tone, and then any alteration. The charts below build on what you already know.

Chords are built starting from a triad and follow a general rule of stacking 3rds from the bottom up: 1–3–5–7–9–11–13.

Major

C, Cmaj, C△	1–3–5
C6, Cmaj6, C△6	1–3–5–6
Cmaj7, C△7	1–3–5–7
Cmaj9, C△9	1–3–5–7–9
Cmaj11, C△11	1–3–5–7–9–11
Cmaj13, C△13	1–3–5–7–9–11–13

Minor

C-, Cm	1–♭3–5
C-6, Cm6	1–♭3–5–6
C-7, Cm7	1–♭3–5–♭7
C-9, Cm9	1–♭3–5–♭7–9
C-11, Cm11	1–♭3–5–♭7–9–11
C-maj7, Cm(maj)7	1–♭3–5–7

Add

With add chords, add the note to an existing triad rather than building a chord all the way up by stacking 3rds. For example, a Cadd9 chord is a C major triad with an added 9th (no 7th is included). A Cadd11 chord is a C major triad with an added 11th (no 7th or 9th).

Cadd9	1-3-5-9
Cadd11	1-3-5-11

Sus

Replace the 3rd with the indicated interval.

Csus2	1-2-5
Csus4	1-4-5

Dominant

A minor 7th, or ♭7, is implied in chord theory when a 7 is present unless indicated as a major 7 (maj7). Dominant chords are built on major triads and include a ♭7. (Note: There can also be a dominant sus chord.)

C7	1-3-5-♭7
C9	1-3-5-♭7-9
C7sus4	1-4-5-♭7
C7sus2	1-2-5-♭7

Diminished and Half-Diminished

A diminished chord is a stack of minor 3rds.

Cdim, C°	1-♭3-♭5
Cdim7, C°7	1-♭3-♭5-♭♭7

A half-diminished chord, or minor 7♭5, is a stack of two minor 3rds with a major 3rd on top.

Cm7♭5, Cø7	1-♭3-♭5-♭7

Augmented

An augmented triad has two major 3rds. An augmented 7th chord adds a ♭7 on top.

C+, Caug	1-3-♯5
C+7, Caug7	1-3-♯5-♭7

FINAL THOUGHTS

Music is a never-ending journey. Even if you stop actively learning, with music it's hard not to evolve. It takes constant practice to keep up with skills at a high level. Like most things, you can lose it if you don't use it, but generally the foundation of musical knowledge and your relationship to hearing and listening deepens with age and time.

Everything in music has a relationship with ear training! We've covered the fundamentals; as you progress and come across new topics, apply the techniques for listening and practice taught in this book. Music is about sound and listening. Whatever area of music you practice, internalize the sound.

At some point, the musical journey leads to do-it-yourself discovery. Hopefully, this book helps you on your musical path. We live in a time when information is at our fingertips. Knowledge is available and accessible. The pace at which life proceeds can be overwhelming, but you can direct that pace. Remember to breathe and slow down when you need to. Discovery can be as deep as you allow yourself to go. It's up to you to get the most out of your experience.

I'd like to dedicate this book to three exceptional musicians who have passed in the last few years. All three of them were examples of musicians with a crazy good ear. They raised the bar for everyone they worked with. Thank you Thomas More Ford, Sean Malone, and Sean Reinert. You will be missed.

"Life is 10% what happens to you and 90% how you react to it."—Charles R. Swindoll

Do-It-Yourself Series

Written especially for adult learners, Do-It-Yourself books:

- Guarantee self-teaching success with thorough explanations and demonstrations
- Use popular songs from the Beatles and Bowie to Taylor Swift and ZZ Top!
- Feature professional video lessons in instrument books to demonstrate key concepts
- Include online audio demos that let you slow down and speed up as needed, loop parts you want to focus on, and more!

TO SEE FULL DESCRIPTIONS OF ALL THE BOOKS IN THE SERIES, VISIT:

halleonard.com